THE COMMANDED BLESSING

David S. Philemon

Royal Diadem Publishing Inc.

Published by David S. Philemon and Royal Diadem Publishing Inc.

The Commanded Blessing
978-1-966141-20-4

For permissions, additional information, or bulk order inquiries, please contact the author.

Write:
Royal Diadem Publishing Inc.
4836 W. 13th Street, Cicero, IL 60804
1 (312) 970-0183

Unless otherwise indicated, all Scripture quotations in this volume are taken from the King James Version (KJV) and the New King James Version (NKJV) of the Holy Bible.

Dedication

To the Almighty God, my foundation and ever-present help. I am grateful for Your boundless love and grace that sustain me daily. And to my mentor in ministry, Rev. George Izunwa, whose steadfast commitment to the call of God has deeply impacted my life. Your guidance and support have been invaluable, encouraging me to walk boldly in the path God has set before me. Thank you for your example and your heart for the Kingdom.

ACKNOWLEDGMENTS

This book would not have been possible without the unwavering support, dedication, and talent of an extraordinary team. My deepest gratitude goes to each of you for your contributions, insights, and encouragement throughout this journey.

First and foremost, thank you to Rev. Mimi Philemon my dear wife, Rev. Shina Gentry, and and my assistant pastor Rev. Bright Amudoaghan for your incredible effort, encouragement, and belief in this project. Your support has been instrumental in bringing this vision to life.

To the dedicated leaders of Royal Diadem Publishing, Ide Imogie and Kishawna Bailey, I am immensely grateful for your belief in this project from the very beginning and for investing your time and energy into its development. Your creativity, dedication, and expertise have been the backbone of this endeavor.

I am especially grateful to the Royal Diadem Publishing team—Beulah Orogun, Emmanuella Ben-Eboh, Doyinsade Awodele, Kim Matthews, and Shante Gill, for your meticulous attention to detail, refining every page and ensuring that each word reflects our vision.

A heartfelt thank you to my family, friends, and colleagues whose unwavering support and belief in this project gave me the courage and strength to see it through.

Finally, thank you to all the readers and supporters who make this work meaningful. I am humbled and honored to share this journey with each of you.

With all my gratitude,
David Philemon

CONTENTS

INTRODUCTION

A commanded blessing is not just a wish or a hope; it's an authorization. Imagine standing before a locked treasure chest, unable to access it, until someone with authority hands you the key and says, "Here, take it. I'm authorizing you to access what's inside." This happens when a spiritual leader, empowered by God, invokes His blessings upon you. They authorize your destiny to access previously unreachable realms.

When God commands His blessings, He releases a divine order. Spiritual leaders, raised by God, grant you the right to step into favor, fortune, and grace, overcoming contradictions. This authorization empowers your destiny to rise, soar, and conquer. It invites you to take up wings like an eagle, develop spiritual strength, and move forward in power.

God Himself says, *"I will make you a new, sharp threshing instrument with teeth"* (Isaiah 41:15, NKJV). This blessing transforms you, enabling you to thrive, confront feared mountains, and shrink them under its power. With this blessing, you walk toward challenges with authority, grinding mountains and hills into dust.

The commanded blessing shifts your destiny, empowering and elevating you to walk in victory. It fills you with confidence, knowing God has authorized your success. This book explores understanding, receiving, and walking in the fullness of this divine authorization.

CHAPTER ONE

THE COMMANDED BLESSING AND PROPHETIC OIL

The commanded blessing is not just a casual statement or prayer. Prophetic oil comes upon a person when a prophet speaks over them, releasing divine authority and favor. This oil makes the impossible possible, unlocking gates and breaking barriers that no human effort could overcome. When a prophet declares a word over your life, it's as if God Himself has anointed you for victory, just as He did for Cyrus.
In Isaiah 45, we see this. God says of Cyrus, "*Whom I have anointed.*" And because of this anointing, God promises to open the two-leaved gates for him, which no man could force open on his own. These were the gates of Babylon, the most fortified gates on earth then. When Isaiah prophesied this, it seemed impossible. People likely questioned how such a thing could happen. Yet Isaiah boldly declared what he saw in the Spirit because the anointing makes the impossible real.

When the commanded blessing is upon you, God goes before you to level mountains, shatter brass gates, and break iron bars. These are not just poetic words. They represent real spiritual and physical obstacles that would stop any ordinary person. But under the commanded blessing, the things others fear and struggle with become your stepping stones. What terrifies others becomes something you trample underfoot with ease.

The anointing doesn't just break through gates; it gives you treasures hidden in darkness. These are the riches, opportunities, and breakthroughs concealed from others. While others labor, struggle, and strive to reach them, you easily access them because the commanded blessing has been released over your life. It's like a divine code that unlocks what was once inaccessible.

God doesn't just open doors for you; He gives you the wisdom to navigate life with divine precision. Wisdom, as we see in the life of Solomon, is a critical element of the commanded blessing. Solomon's life reflected Psalm 112, where the man who delights in the Lord is blessed beyond measure. Wisdom allowed Solomon to rule, judge, and access riches and honor in ways others could not. His wisdom wasn't just a gift for himself but a demonstration of God's favor over his life.

The same wisdom is available to you under the commanded blessing. It allows you to go through life with less struggle, avoiding traps and pitfalls that others fall into. It gives you insight into which doors are genuinely from God and which are snares laid by the enemy. Not every open door is from God, and not every closed door is an obstacle. Sometimes, God closes doors to protect you from harm or preserve what belongs to you from those who steal it.

The commanded blessing removes competition from your life. Like Joseph in Egypt or Daniel in Babylon, no one could compete with the favor of God in their lives. Joseph didn't just interpret dreams; he unlocked mysteries no one else could. Daniel didn't just solve riddles; he entered the spiritual realm and brought answers that confounded the wisest men of his time. This is what the commanded blessing does: it places you in a league where no one else can match what God is doing in your life.

But this blessing comes with responsibility. God warns that we will pay the price if we take His work for granted. Neglected altars lead to generational consequences. When the altar of your life is neglected, God says He will rebuke your children. To rebuke means to reject and remove the honor He once placed upon them. It's not enough to receive the commanded blessing; we must cherish it, nurture it, and ensure that the altar of our lives remains active and burning with God's fire.

Honor doesn't come because we demand it. It comes because God places it upon us. When we neglect the source of that honor, the altar, we open the door for dishonor and shame to enter our and our children's lives. God says He will spread the manure of animals, the very waste of sacrifices, on the faces of those who dishonor Him, treating them like refuse. This is when blessings turn to sorrow, and what was meant to elevate us brings shame because we failed to honor the Giver of the blessing.

Solomon, though he received everything on a silver platter, understood the weight of the commanded blessing. His life was a manifestation of Psalm 112, where those who cherish the word of God are blessed beyond measure. Solomon's wisdom allowed him to rule with excellence, navigate complex issues quickly, and bring honor to the name of God. But even Solomon understood that this blessing had to be nurtured. He built altars, offered sacrifices, and remained faithful to God, ensuring that the blessing remained active in his life.

The commanded blessing exceeds our expectations. When it rests upon you, you don't have to fear losing anything good that God has given you. It erases competition, giving you an edge in every area of life. Whether in business, ministry, or personal relationships, God places you ahead of the competition because His favor is upon you. This cannot be earned or worked for; it is a gift that comes through God's prophetic declaration and anointing.

Divine wisdom accompanies the commanded blessing. This wisdom allows you to access earthly treasures and spiritual insights others cannot see. Daniel's ability to dream the king's dream before interpreting it exceeded human understanding. This kind of wisdom comes with the commanded blessing: the ability to see into the spiritual realm, understand things hidden from others and bring solutions that no one else can provide.

As we walk in the commanded blessing, we must also walk in wisdom. Not every battle is meant to be fought. Some doors are closed for a reason, and some battles are distractions from the actual fight. Wisdom helps us discern which opportunities to pursue and which to let go. It allows us to recognize the difference between God's open doors and the enemy's traps. This is essential for living under the commanded blessing because not every glittering opportunity is from God, and not every closed door is a denial.

God's wisdom also protects us from the schemes of the enemy. Sometimes, He closes doors to keep wicked people from accessing what belongs to us. Just as He protected Solomon's kingdom with wisdom, He will protect your life, family, and destiny through the same divine insight. But we must remain connected to the altar, ensuring our relationship with God remains active and vibrant.

Finally, the commanded blessing is not just a statement but a powerful force that changes everything in your life. It opens doors, shatters obstacles, and gives you access to hidden treasures. But it requires honor, wisdom, and a commitment to maintaining the altar of your life. As you walk under this blessing, may you experience the fullness of God's favor, wisdom, and protection, knowing that no competition can remove you from where God has positioned you.

The Reflection Of Blessing – Seed, Womb, And Wisdom

As we step into the commanded blessing, we must grasp how God's blessings manifest in the natural and spiritual realms. When God blesses, He doesn't just meet your expectations; He exceeds them beyond anything you could imagine. This is not merely a promise but a reflection of His nature, where blessings flow from generation to generation, impacting not only your children but also the works of your hands, your businesses, and everything birthed from your efforts.

As seen in Malachi 2:2, when blessings turn to curses, God's rebuke extends to your descendants, removing favor and honor from their lives. This rebuke affects everything that springs from your biological and spiritual seed. Your "children" don't always have to be from your physical lineage; they could be the businesses you birth, the ministries you start, or even dreams you partner with others to bring forth. Anything from your effort or collaboration can carry the seed of blessing or curse, depending on your obedience to God.

Seed And Womb In Destiny

We often think of reproduction in terms of biological children, but in the realm of destiny, this process takes on a much broader meaning. Men carry the seed, and women receive it, but in life's spiritual journey, sometimes you carry the seed of an idea, a vision, or a dream. Other times, you are the womb that receives and nurtures someone else's dream until it is brought to fruition.

In the natural order, for a seed to bring forth life, it must be planted in fertile soil. Similarly, your dreams, businesses, and ideas must be planted in environments conducive to growth. Solomon, for instance, received wisdom as a seed from God. It was planted in him and bore much fruit, as evidenced by his wealth, influence, and the glory of his reign.

However, the story of Solomon also teaches us a vital lesson: when a seed is planted in contaminated soil, the outcome is equally tainted. Solomon's wisdom became corrupted by the women in his life, leading him to stray from God's commandments. This shows us that even the greatest blessings, when not carefully guarded, can be derailed by the wrong influences.

Just as Solomon's wisdom initially attracted the admiration of others, it eventually led to his downfall because he allowed those who did not honor God to influence him. Be mindful of who you let into your life because not everyone who admires your wisdom, success, or blessings is there to support you. Some are there to corrupt what God has placed within you.

In a vision, God revealed to me the nature of His wisdom. He appeared as wisdom itself, and I saw Him take on multiple forms. His presence was unchanging yet ever-evolving, showing me that true wisdom is dynamic, able to adapt and apply itself in various circumstances without losing its essence.

As I breathed in His fragrance, it filled the atmosphere, transforming the environment around me. This is the power of God's wisdom; it changes everything it touches. Just as a fragrance fills a room, divine wisdom permeates every aspect of our lives, from our decisions to our relationships, and it brings about a supernatural shift in our circumstances.

When I had this encounter, God reminded me of a dream in which I wore a fragrance I hadn't used in years. The scent symbolized wisdom, and He instructed me to wear it again. This fragrance was not just a physical scent but a spiritual mantle of wisdom that God placed upon me.

The lesson here is clear: the wisdom God gives you will distinguish you, making you a sign and wonder to your generation. Just as Solomon's wisdom attracted the Queen of Sheba, so too will God's wisdom upon you draw the attention of kings and queens, leaders and influencers. But, just as Solomon's wisdom was tested, so will yours be.

The Queen of Sheba came to test Solomon with hard questions because she respected his wisdom. In life, you will face similar tests. People will come into your life to see how deep, pure, and resilient you genuinely carry wisdom. These tests are not to be feared; God ordains them to refine you and ensure that the blessings He has placed upon your life are built on a solid foundation.

However, there is a difference between a God-ordained test and a temptation. Solomon's downfall came not from the Queen of Sheba's test but from the temptations of the women in his life. They admired his wisdom initially, but they introduced foreign gods and influences that corrupted his heart over time.

Be vigilant in your relationships, for not everyone who enters your life has pure motives. Some may test your wisdom, while others seek to tempt you from God's path.

Consider King Solomon's experience. The women in his life didn't initially lead him astray. Instead, they subtly requested financial support for their shrines, saying, "*You don't have to come; just give us the money, and we'll take care of it.*" What seemed like a minor compromise eventually led Solomon down a destructive path, causing him to worship their gods.

We must learn from Solomon's mistake. The small, seemingly insignificant compromises often lead to the greatest downfalls. Guard your heart, for out of it flows the wellspring of life. Test every spirit, as the Bible instructs us, and do not be afraid to challenge the motives of those around you. This testing is not to trap or manipulate but to discern whether the relationship is built on a foundation of truth and righteousness.

The Power Of Wisdom To Navigate Life's Complications

One of the greatest blessings of the commanded blessing is the ability to navigate life's most complicated situations with divine wisdom. The Bible says in James 1:5 that if anyone lacks wisdom, they should ask of God, who gives generously to all without finding fault.

Wisdom is more than just knowledge or understanding. It is the ability to apply God's truth to every situation, no matter how complex. It helps you see beyond the surface and understand the spiritual implications of your decisions.

I declare that you are receiving a special kind of wisdom right now. This wisdom will empower you to make decisions that others cannot understand. It will set you apart and elevate you to a place of influence and authority. Just as Solomon was known for his wisdom, so will you become a sign and wonder to your generation.

As the commanded blessing rests upon you, God will allow you to navigate the dark places in life. Whether in your business, relationships, or ministry, God's wisdom will lead you through every challenge and bring you to victory.

Don't forget that the commanded blessing is not just for you; it’s for your descendants, businesses, and everything that comes from you. Just as Solomon’s wisdom and prosperity extended to his descendants, so will God’s blessing extend to every part of your life. But be vigilant. Guard your heart, test every spirit, and be mindful of the relationships you allow into your life.

May God’s wisdom fill your life like a sweet fragrance, transforming every atmosphere you walk into. May you carry this mantle with honor, and may the commanded blessing bring you into a place of influence, prosperity, and favor that exceeds your wildest expectations.

The Power Of The Commanded Blessing

The commanded blessing is not an ordinary blessing. It is a divine instruction that, when released, brings supernatural provision and abundance. In Leviticus 25, God speaks to His people about a unique blessing in the sixth year, enabling them to rest in the seventh year without lack. This is not just about crops or land; it is a principle that applies to every aspect of life, whether it be your business, career, or finances. The commanded blessing brings security and prosperity and is enough to sustain you beyond your wildest expectations.

Leviticus 25:21 says, "Then I will command My blessing on you in the sixth year, and it will bring forth produce enough for three years." Imagine that! One year of labor yields three years of provision. God says that when He commands a blessing, it overrides the natural order. You may work today, but God's blessing will sustain you for years. This blessing positions you to live in abundance without fear of tomorrow.

Now, let's explore how this commanded blessing functions. When God releases it, there is a supernatural multiplication of resources. It's as if everything you touch flourishes beyond what is naturally possible. Whether in business, working a job, or managing a household, this blessing ensures you survive and thrive.

The commanded blessing doesn't just affect one area of your life; it touches everything. Your business, your family, and even your children benefit from it. When the Bible speaks of blessed descendants, it's not just about biological children. It also refers to anything that comes from you, your business, your ideas, your work. They are like your offspring, and God's blessing ensures that they will prosper.

Consider this: your business can be like a child. It was born from your hard work; like any child, it needs nurturing. But the commanded blessing guarantees that what you have birthed will not just survive but will flourish. This is not just about financial prosperity but also about influence and impact. When the blessing rests on your business, it becomes a platform for more incredible things, favor, expansion, and growth beyond what you could imagine.

God is not limited by time, space, or resources. When He releases a blessing, it transcends the natural limitations. You may be concerned about what will happen next year or how your business will survive a tough season, but God is already ahead of you. He has commanded a blessing to care for the future; you will not have to worry about lack.

The Importance Of Obedience

The commanded blessings come with a condition: obedience. In Leviticus, God instructed His people to rest in the seventh year, trusting that He would provide for them—this required faith. Many work themselves to exhaustion in our fast-paced world, never resting in God's provision. But the principle here is clear: obedience unlocks the blessing. You position yourself to receive His supernatural provision when you follow God's instructions, even when they seem illogical or complex.

Rest is not just about ceasing from work but about trusting God. It's about knowing He works on your behalf even when you are not. When God commanded the Israelites to rest, it was a test of their faith. Would they trust Him to provide for them, or would they try to make things happen independently? The same question applies to us today. Will we trust God enough to rest, knowing His blessing will cover us?

The commanded blessing is a demonstration of God's faithfulness. He doesn't just give enough for today but more than enough to sustain you in the future. This blessing allows you to step into new levels of prosperity without striving or struggling. It is a blessing that carries you through seasons of uncertainty and stabilizes every area of your life.

Supernatural Wisdom And Favor

One of the critical elements of the commanded blessing is the release of supernatural wisdom and favor. When God blesses you, He allows you to navigate difficult situations easily. You don't just survive challenges; you thrive in them because God gives you the wisdom to make the right decisions.

Consider Solomon, who was blessed with wisdom beyond measure. The Bible says that people came from worldwide just to hear his wisdom. This wisdom was part of God's commanded blessing on his life. It brought him wealth, influence, and favor. However, we must remember Solomon's downfall when he allowed external influences to corrupt the blessing. The women in his life led him astray, causing him to worship other gods. This teaches us that while the commanded blessing brings great favor, it also requires us to guard it carefully.

Wisdom is one of the most valuable aspects of the commanded blessing. It allows you to make decisions that lead to prosperity and influence. When you operate under the commanded blessing, God gives you insight into things others cannot see. You may be facing a tough decision in your business, but God will provide you with the wisdom to handle it successfully. You may be struggling with a relationship, but the knowledge that comes with the commanded blessing will help you handle it gracefully.

Multiplication And Abundance

The commanded blessing also brings multiplication. When God blesses something, it doesn't just grow; it multiplies. Just as in Leviticus, where one year of labor produced enough for three years, God can multiply what you have beyond what you thought was possible. This is not just about material wealth; it's about influence, favor, and impact. When God multiplies your efforts, you find yourself accomplishing more in less time, with less effort.

This is the power of the commanded blessing. It accelerates things. What would take others years to achieve, you will accomplish in months. What would take others months? You will do it in days. This is not because of your strength or ability but because of God's blessing in your life. He is the one who multiplies your efforts and brings about supernatural results.

You cannot earn the commanded blessing; it is a gift from God. However, it requires obedience and faith. You must trust that God will provide for you, even when it seems impossible. You must rest in His provision, knowing He has already commanded a blessing over your life.

As you walk in obedience and faith, you will see the fruit of the commanded blessing in every area of your life. Your business and relationships will flourish, and you will experience abundance beyond your wildest dreams. This is the power of the commanded blessing; it goes beyond what you can do in your strength and brings supernatural provision and favor. From now on, may you walk in the commanded blessing. May you experience the multiplication of your efforts and the release of mystical wisdom. May God's favor rest upon you, and may you never lack. The commanded blessing is upon you and will sustain you for years. Amen.

CHAPTER TWO

UNLOCKING THE COMMANDED BLESSING THROUGH OBEDIENCE

Obedience is a critical key to unlocking the commanded blessing. In Leviticus 25, God profoundly reveals how His blessing operates through obedience. He said, "If you obey, I will command My blessing upon you in the sixth year, and it shall bring forth fruit for three years." This is not just an ordinary blessing but a commanded one, a blessing that overflows beyond the boundaries of the expected.

Let's break this down. The commanded blessing doesn't just provide for you in the current season; it stretches into future seasons. God promised His blessing would be so powerful in the sixth year that it would sustain you for the seventh, eighth, and even ninth year. Imagine that kind of abundance! Even when the new crops of the following year come in, you will still have enough from the previous years. This is the power of the commanded blessing.

God's blessings are meant to transcend time and natural circumstances. In Leviticus 25:21, He says, "*I will command my blessing upon you in the sixth year, and it shall bring forth fruit for three years.*" This is no ordinary harvest. God's commanded blessing is not limited to just one season or year; it is a supernatural provision that carries you through multiple seasons, ensuring you are never in lack.

It's important to understand that this blessing is not just about crops for the Israelites. For us today, this extends to every area of life: businesses, finances, careers, opportunities, and even relationships. The commanded blessing means that God will give you such an overflow that you will still thrive even when others are struggling or experiencing drought. In modern terms, this could be compared to having abundant financial reserves; even if you don't work for two or three years, you still live comfortably and in prosperity.

But here's the key: this blessing is tied to obedience. God clearly states, "If you obey..." Obedience unlocks the door to the commanded blessing. It's not just about going to church or doing religious activities; it's about surrendering to God's instructions. When God gives a command, He's not just speaking for the sake of it; He is releasing divine direction that can shift your life into realms of overflow.

Many people miss out on the fullness of God's blessing because they choose partial or delayed obedience, which is disobedience. But God is looking for those who will respond immediately to His word and walk in alignment with His will. When we do this, we position ourselves to receive the commanded blessing that flows beyond the natural limitations of time, space, or resources.

Rest And Renewal: A Command To Receive

Another critical aspect of unlocking the blessing of God is understanding the profound principle of rest. In Leviticus 25, God explicitly instructed His people about the rhythm of work and rest, commanding them to work for six years and rest in the seventh year. What stands out is the assurance that follows this command: God promises His people that they should not worry about what they will eat or how they will survive during the seventh year. Why? Because the blessing He commands during the sixth year will be sufficient to sustain them through the seventh.

This passage teaches us something deeply profound about the rhythm God has ordained for rest and reliance on Him. Rest is not just about taking a break from physical labor; it is a form of trust and dependence on God's provision. Sadly, many believers today are caught up in a constant cycle of endless work, striving to make ends meet, working daily without pause, often driven by the fear of lack or the need to stay ahead. This pattern reflects a mindset that assumes it's up to human effort alone to meet every need. But God's design for His people goes beyond striving. It's about trusting Him enough to rest and receive from His commanded blessing.

The kind of rest God desires for us is not about laziness or inactivity. The opposite is about a purposeful pause that brings spiritual renewal and deep reliance on God's grace. When we engage in this form of rest, we are reminded that our ability to sustain ourselves is limited, and God ultimately provides. Rest becomes an act of faith, a reminder that God's blessing can do more than we could ever accomplish through sheer human effort.

Entering into God's rest is also a spiritual discipline. It's about shifting our mindset from relentless self-reliance to one anchored in divine dependence. When we honor God by resting, we make a powerful declaration: "I trust that You are my provider." This kind of faith is essential to unlock the fullness of God's blessing because it moves us out of the driver's seat and places God in the center of our lives. Rest, in this sense, becomes a powerful act of worship. It communicates to God that we believe He can meet our needs, even when we pause from our labor.

It's crucial to recognize that rest isn't just about physical rejuvenation. Rest also involves the renewal of our minds, spirits, and hearts. In our fast-paced world, many people equate productivity with worth and believe they fail if they aren't constantly busy. But this mindset robs us of the peace and blessing God desires to pour into our lives. Rest is about ceasing from our works to make space for God's work in us. Hebrews 4:10 reminds us of this when it says, "For he who has entered His rest has also ceased from his works as God did from His."

When we rest, we invite God's blessing to flow more freely into our lives. It allows us to stop striving and start receiving. Rest positions us to hear God's voice more clearly and to experience His provision more fully. The children of Israel had to trust that God would indeed provide in the sixth year to sustain them through the seventh. This required faith and obedience; they had to stop working and trust that God would honor His word. Similarly, when we rest, we must trust that God's commanded blessing is enough to carry us through.

Another important aspect of rest is its connection to worship. By setting aside time to rest, we are not simply taking a break for physical recovery. We are acknowledging that God is our source and sustainer. Rest is an act of worship; it's a way of declaring to God that our hope is not in our abilities but His power and provision. In Exodus 16, God provided manna for the Israelites in the wilderness, but He commanded them to gather twice as much on the sixth day because there would be none to gather on the seventh. Here again, we see the principle of trust and rest; God provided enough in advance to sustain them through their day of rest.

Today, many believers struggle with rest because they have placed their security in the work of their hands rather than in the hands of God. They labor without ceasing, afraid that everything will fall apart if they stop. But rest, as outlined in scripture, is not about abandoning responsibility. Instead, it's about embracing a higher truth: God's blessing, when commanded, is more than enough to sustain us. In Matthew 6:31-33, Jesus speaks to this very issue, saying, "Do not worry, saying, 'What shall we eat?' or 'What shall we drink?' or 'What shall we wear?' For your heavenly Father knows that you need these things. But seek the kingdom of God and His righteousness first, and all these things shall be added to you."

God wants His people to be diligent in their work, but He also wants them to rest in His sufficiency. By establishing the principle of rest, God reminds us that it is not by our strength or our might. Still, by His Spirit, we are sustained (Zechariah 4:6). It's a reminder that when we honor God's command to rest, He honors His promise to bless us abundantly. It is not wrong to work hard and be diligent, but it is equally important to celebrate the rhythm God has set for our lives by taking time to rest and renew our spirits.

In practical terms, resting does not mean we are idle or inactive. It means we take deliberate steps to recharge and refocus our hearts on God's purpose. Rest may involve stepping away from work-related tasks, but it also means setting aside time to spend with God, to meditate on His word, and to be refreshed by His presence. During these rest times, we often receive more profound insights and clarity. Rest positions us to hear from God and gain the strength to carry on with renewed vigor.

The principle of rest also speaks to the issue of sustainability. Without rest, we burn out. We lose focus, become frustrated, and start to operate out of fear or anxiety rather than faith. Rest ensures that we are continually operating in the strength and power of God rather than in our limited capacity. In Leviticus 25, God's commanded blessing during the sixth year was enough to carry His people through the seventh year. This teaches us that human timelines or work schedules do not limit God's provision. When He commands a blessing, it is sufficient to meet every need.

The Spirit Of Vashti: Pride And Disobedience

A great example of the consequences of disobedience is found in the story of Vashti in the book of Esther. Vashti was the queen, married to King Ahasuerus, who ruled over a vast kingdom. During a grand feast, the king summoned her to appear before his guests to display her beauty. However, in her pride and arrogance, she refused to obey the king's command. Instead of submitting to his request, she chose to please her desires and possibly the opinions of those around her. This act of defiance and disobedience cost Vashti the crown and her position as queen.

Vashti's story illustrates the dangers that pride and disobedience bring into one's life. When you refuse to obey divine instructions, or in Vashti's case, a royal command, you risk losing what God has entrusted you. Vashti had the incredible privilege of being the queen, a position of honor and authority. However, her pride made her forget the magnitude of her role and responsibilities. In the same way, when believers operate in pride, ignoring their dependence on God and His grace, they block the flow of His commanded blessing.

Vashti's refusal to honor the king's request can be seen as symbolic of how pride often makes us blind to the consequences of our actions. Pride makes us believe that we are in control, do not need to submit to any higher authority and know what is best for our lives. But as Vashti's story shows, this mindset leads to a fall. Scripture tells us in Proverbs 16:18, "Pride goes before destruction and a haughty spirit before a fall." Vashti's disobedience serves as a warning to all believers that pride can cause us to lose the very things God has given us.

The story of Vashti is a vivid reminder that positions of favor, influence, and authority come with responsibilities. Vashti's role as queen was not just about her beauty or status; it was a position of influence and trust God gave her. However, when pride takes over, we often forget that these roles and blessings are not for our selfish gain but for God's purposes. Vashti failed to see that her refusal to obey the king was an act of rebellion against her husband and a failure to fulfill her duty as queen. She neglected the larger picture and the responsibility that came with her position.

The spirit of Vashti is still at work today, causing people to prioritize pleasing others or their desires over obeying God. How often have we chosen to go our own way, ignoring God's instructions because we think we know better or want to please the people around us? Like Vashti, we sometimes fail to recognize that obedience to God is not optional but a command. And when we disobey, we risk losing the very things that God has entrusted to us, whether our influence, our position, or even His favor.

One of the critical lessons from Vashti's story is that pride makes us forget our place and dependence on God. Vashti's pride made her think she was untouchable and could make decisions without consequences. But in doing so, she lost her position. Likewise, pride can make us forget our place before God, leading us to believe we are self-sufficient. This is dangerous because the blessings and positions of favor in our lives are not a result of our efforts; they are a result of God's grace. When we forget this and begin to operate in pride, we cut ourselves off from the source of blessing.

The commanded blessing, the flow of divine favor and provision, can only be accessed through humility and obedience. Pride will always push us away from the place of blessing. The Bible contains examples of individuals who lost their place of favor because of pride. Lucifer's fall from heaven is one of the most prominent examples of how pride can lead to destruction. He, too, was privileged, but his pride made him rebel against God, and he lost his place.

In contrast, humility allows God's blessing to flow into our lives.

When we humble ourselves and submit to God's instructions, we place ourselves in a position to receive His favor. James 4:6 says, "God resists the proud but gives grace to the humble." Humility is the key to unlocking the commanded blessing. It acknowledges that everything we have comes from God and recognizes that we depend on His provision, guidance, and grace.

Vashti's downfall also teaches us that obedience to authority is crucial in maintaining the blessing. God often works through the authorities He has placed over us, whether that be spiritual, governmental, or relational authority. When we rebel against these authorities, we also rebel against God's order. Vashti's rebellion against the king can be seen as a parallel to our rebellion against God when we choose to go our way. Just as Vashti's disobedience cost her the crown, our disobedience to God's commands can cost us the blessings He has prepared for us.

Moreover, Vashti wanted to show her friends that she was in control, but in doing so, she lost her position. The spirit of Vashti causes people to prioritize their image and the opinions of others over God's will. This is a dangerous path because seeking the approval of others often leads us away from obedience to God. In Galatians 1:10, Paul says, "For am I now seeking the approval of man, or God? Or am I trying to please man? If I were still trying to please man, I would not be a servant of Christ." Pleasing people instead of obeying God will always lead us away from the place of blessing.

Esther: The Power Of Divine Alignment

In contrast to Vashti's downfall through pride and disobedience, we are introduced to Esther, a woman who exemplifies the power of divine alignment. Esther was not the most powerful woman in Persia, nor was she of noble birth. Yet, through obedience and humility, she found favor in the sight of God and man. Esther's rise to the position of queen was not due to her striving but because she aligned herself with God's purpose and timing. This story offers a powerful lesson on the importance of divine alignment in unlocking the commanded blessing.

From the beginning, Esther understood the value of submission and spiritual preparation. She was raised by her cousin Mordecai after being orphaned, and it was his wisdom and instruction that Esther respected and followed. Mordecai played an essential role in guiding her through the complexities of life in the Persian Empire. Unlike Vashti, who disregarded the counsel of others, Esther positioned herself by aligning with Mordecai's wisdom. This alignment with godly instruction would later open the door for Esther to become queen and, ultimately, a vessel of deliverance for her people.

Esther's rise to prominence was not by chance but because of her outward beauty. The Bible tells us that when Esther was chosen to be part of the king's harem, she did not demand special treatment or privilege like the other women. Instead, she humbly followed the advice of Hegai, the custodian of the women, choosing only what he recommended for her beautification. This is a crucial example of how Esther understood the importance of being in the right place at the right time and aligning with the right people. Her humility and obedience brought her favor in the sight of the king and everyone who saw her. It was this attitude of divine alignment that positioned her to become queen.

Once Esther became queen, she didn't allow the privilege of her position to make her complacent. She remained connected to Mordecai and continued to receive counsel from him. When Mordecai uncovered Haman's plot to destroy the Jewish people, he sent a message to Esther, urging her to intercede on behalf of their people. Esther faced a critical decision. She could have easily ignored Mordecai's plea, enjoying her life in the palace while her people perished. However, Esther understood that her position was not for personal gain but for a greater purpose. This reveals a powerful principle: divine alignment always serves a higher purpose.

Esther's response to Mordecai's message is a testament to her spiritual maturity. She did not rush into the king's presence out of fear or panic. Instead, she called for a three-day fast, seeking God's guidance before moving. This shows the depth of Esther's understanding that accurate alignment with God's plan requires preparation, prayer, and a dependence on divine wisdom. Esther knew that success would not come from her status as queen but from her alignment with God's will. This act of fasting demonstrates that spiritual alignment involves setting aside time to seek God's direction before making critical decisions.

When the time came for Esther to approach the king, she did so with courage and confidence, knowing that God was backing her every move. Esther's boldness in going before the king without being summoned could have cost her life, as it was against the law. However, Esther recognized that aligning with God's plan sometimes requires taking risks. She said, "If I perish, I perish," demonstrating that she was willing to sacrifice her life to fulfill God's purpose. This boldness comes only from the assurance that you are in divine alignment.

Esther's story teaches us that divine alignment involves spiritual preparation and courage. It requires being in tune with God's timing and purpose, even when it means stepping out of our comfort zone. Esther did not allow fear to hold her back from doing what needed to be done. Instead, she relied on the strength and wisdom from aligning herself with God's will. Her obedience and courage led to the king extending his golden scepter, granting her favor and access. This moment signifies how divine alignment opens doors no human effort can achieve.

Once Esther had gained the king's favor, she did not hastily present her request to him. She invited the king and Haman to a banquet, exercising patience and discernment. This shows that divine alignment also involves strategic timing. Esther did not rush the process; she trusted that God was orchestrating the events in her favor. Her patience and wisdom in handling the situation ultimately led to Haman's downfall and the Jewish people's deliverance.

Esther's story exemplifies how aligning with God's purpose brings about the commanded blessing. She was not born into a position of power, nor did she strive to become queen through her efforts. Instead, she aligned herself with divine instruction, respected the authority in her life, and remained sensitive to God's timing. Through her obedience, humility, and courage, Esther secured the blessing for herself and her entire nation.

One of the key takeaways from Esther's life is that divine alignment requires a heart of humility and a willingness to serve a purpose greater than oneself. Esther could have easily used her position for personal gain or to enjoy the luxuries of palace life. However, she recognized that her position was divinely appointed for a specific purpose: to be a vessel of deliverance for her people. In the same way, when we align ourselves with God's will, we position ourselves to be used for His glory and the benefit of others.

Another vital lesson from Esther's story is the importance of patience and timing. Esther did not rush ahead of God's plan or try to manipulate the situation to her advantage. She understood that divine alignment requires waiting on God's timing, trusting He will bring about the desired outcome in His way. This principle is vital for believers who want to walk in the commanded blessing. We must learn to wait on God's timing and trust that He is working behind the scenes, even when we cannot see the whole picture.

Commanding The Blessing Through Spiritual Authority

As believers, we must understand that the commanded blessing doesn't fall into our laps. It requires spiritual authority and an understanding of divine principles. Just as Mordecai taught Esther, we need spiritual mentors and teachers to guide us into the more profound things of God. We must learn spiritual technicalities to activate the commanded blessing in our lives.

We must understand the power of altars, prayer, fasting, and obedience to God's word. These are the tools that establish the commanded blessing in our lives. When we take spiritual matters seriously and engage in these practices, we create an environment where the blessing can flow without hindrance.

Just as Esther's obedience led to Haman's downfall and her people's deliverance, our obedience can unlock victories, breakthroughs, and blessings beyond our imagination.

The commanded blessing is available to every believer, but it is accessed through obedience, humility, and a deep understanding of spiritual principles. When we align ourselves with God's will and walk in His ways, we position ourselves to receive a blessing that overflows into every area of our lives: finances, health, relationships, and more.

God desires to display His goodness through you, just as the king wanted to display the beauty of his queen. But you must wear the royal garments of obedience, humility, and faith. As you do this, God will command His blessing upon you, sustaining you through every season and bringing you into a place of supernatural abundance and provision.

The Spirit Of Error And The Consequence Of Neglecting Spiritual Altars

Some doors open with great opportunities, blessings, and

breakthroughs. Still, even with these open doors, if there is an altar fighting against you, it contradicts those opportunities and hinders your progress. No matter how grand the opportunities may seem if the altar that opposes you is not addressed, it will rise to block and frustrate the cloud of blessings assigned to your life.

Consider the case of Solomon's son, Rehoboam. He inherited a powerful kingdom that could have flourished under his rule. Yet, a contradictory prophecy hangs over his life, one that he pays no attention to. He neglected the spiritual maintenance of his altar, and because of this neglect, the spirit of error hijacks his kingdom. The prophet had already forewarned his father Solomon in 1 Kings 11, but Solomon's refusal to heed the warnings eventually led to the downfall of his lineage.

Solomon's downfall began with his disobedience. The Bible records that Solomon, though blessed with wisdom and wealth, allowed his heart to be swayed by foreign women. 1 Kings 11:1-2 says, "King Solomon loved many foreign women, along with the daughter of Pharaoh—women of the Moabites, Ammonites, Edomites, Sidonians, and Hittites." These were nations whose people worshiped idols, and the Lord had explicitly instructed the Israelites not to intermarry with them, knowing the danger this posed to their spiritual lives.

Despite the warning, Solomon married many women from these idolatrous nations. Over time, their influence led him away from worshipping the true God. The Bible says that his heart was turned, and in his old age, he no longer followed God wholly as David, his father, had. Solomon even went so far as to build altars and temples to these false gods, setting up places of worship for the gods of Moab, Ammon, and others on the Mount of Olives, where Jesus would later ascend to heaven.

These actions corrupted his altar. Solomon, a man who God once loved, became the builder of altars for demons. His wisdom became polluted. He lost the divine favor that had once been his.

What was most tragic, however, was the impact on Solomon and his son. God told Solomon, "I will tear the kingdom away from you and give it to one of your subordinates. Nevertheless, for the sake of your father, David, I will not do it during your lifetime. I will take it out of the hand of your son" - 1 Kings 11:11-12.

Solomon's neglect of his altar destroyed the future of his son, Rehoboam. The moment Rehoboam ascended to the throne, trouble ensued. The people came to him, asking for relief from the heavy taxes imposed by Solomon in his later years. Instead of listening to the wisdom of the elders, Rehoboam sought advice from his young friends, who encouraged him to increase the burden on the people. This decision led to the splitting of the kingdom, with Jeroboam, a former servant of Solomon, taking ten tribes and leaving Rehoboam with only one.

The spirit of error hijacked Rehoboam's reign. Instead of ruling wisely, as his grandfather David had, or as his father Solomon once did, Rehoboam allowed pride, arrogance, and poor judgment to lead him astray. He failed to address the altar that his father had corrupted, so he lost almost the entire kingdom.

This is the power of spiritual altars. Whether good or evil, an altar speaks to the destiny of individuals, families, and nations. David had raised a godly altar that secured the future of his lineage, but Solomon corrupted that altar, and his son Rehoboam paid the price.

Some of you today may be fighting battles not of your own making. You may be struggling against altars raised by your forefathers, altars of idolatry, witchcraft, or ungodly covenants. These altars are fighting your destiny, hindering your progress, and blocking the blessings that are rightfully yours. But let me tell you, these altars can be torn down. Just as God gave Solomon the chance to repent and correct his ways, He is allowing you to raise a godly altar in place of the corrupted ones that have plagued your family.

The most merciful thing God did for Solomon was to send the Queen of Sheba to validate his respect for God early in his reign. God was showing Solomon that His way was the best decision Solomon could ever make. But Solomon turned away, and his heart was divided. He ignored God's warnings, and it led to the downfall of his kingdom.

You must be vigilant in maintaining your spiritual altar. The Bible says in Leviticus 6:13, "*A fire shall always be burning on the altar; it shall never go out.*" This means that your altar must be continuously serviced. You cannot afford to let the fire die out. When you neglect your altar, the enemy finds a way in, like the one that overtook Solomon and Rehoboam; the spirit of error begins to operate when your altar is weak.

The enemy does not fight fairly. When you ignore your altar, he raises his. While you are distracted, he works behind the scenes, building altars to snatch away your blessings, opportunities, and even your destiny. But God has given us the power to correct these errors. We can rebuild the altars in our lives, just as Elijah rebuilt the altar that was broken in 1 Kings 18:30.

Elijah's story is a perfect example of the importance of spiritual altars. In his time, the altars of Israel had been neglected, and the people had turned to worship Baal. But Elijah, a man of God, called the people back to the true God by repairing the altar and calling down fire from heaven. When the fire fell, it consumed the sacrifice and demonstrated the power of God. In the same way, when you repair your altar, God's power will be evident in your life.

The spirit of error that pollutes and weakens altars must be dealt with decisively. If left unchecked, it allows negative prophecies to come to pass. Just as Esther was banished and replaced by Vashti, altars of error and disobedience will always lead to displacement. The altars we raise or neglect determine the course of our lives. If your altar is compromised, your destiny will be compromised as well.

You cannot afford to be careless with your altar. Every day, you must serve it with prayer, worship, and obedience to God's word. As Leviticus 6:12-13 reminds us, "And the fire on the altar shall be kept burning on it; it shall not be put out." The fire on your altar must never go out. It is your responsibility to ensure that it remains alive and burning. When your altar is strong, no enemy can prevail against you.

The spirit of error that destroyed Solomon's legacy and crippled Rehoboam's reign will not have a place in your life if you keep your altar burning. Stand firm in your faith, maintain your spiritual altar, and watch God fight your battles and secure your destiny.

The Commanded Deliverance: Breaking Free From Contradictory Prophecies

One of the most powerful functions of the commanded blessing is the commanded deliverance. This is when God's authority breaks the chains that have caged His people, enabling them to walk in the destiny He has prepared for them entirely. Psalm 44:4 in The Passion Translation (TPT) says, "You are my King and my God, who decrees victories for Jacob." When deliverance is commanded, it is not just a casual release from oppression but a royal decree from the King of Kings. This means that whatever has hindered or restricted Jacob (representing God's people) from becoming everything God intends must bow. It must give way to the majesty of the person delivered.

The commanded deliverance comes with majesty because it restores the rightful glory God ordained for your life. There is a glory tied to your name, a manifestation of divine destiny that God is eager to bring forth. When God commands deliverance, He doesn't just stop at setting you free; He ensures that you walk in the fullness of your purpose. You will manifest that glory, and I am here to tell you that you will see that manifestation this month and this year.

God visited me with four Heavenly Beings in preparation for this teaching. These Heavenly Beings, whom I cannot fully describe, carry a powerful presence that signifies the seriousness of the deliverance and breakthrough He has planned for you. This is not just another message; this is a divine appointment. Even the most skeptical person reading this will receive because God is eager to demonstrate His greatness and love.

In the next few weeks, you will find yourself basking in the favor and goodness of God. A new phase of life is upon you. What may have seemed dark or stagnant will suddenly be flooded with the light of God's favor. Your life will be transformed in such a way that it will be like night turning into day. You will know beyond a shadow of a doubt that God has sent me to you and has a specific plan for your life.

Now, let us deal with contradictory prophecies, that is, those situations where a blessing seems to be declared over your life, but opposing forces are at work to derail that blessing. Solomon, the son of King David, is a prime example of how contradictory prophecies can influence one's destiny. Solomon inherited immense glory, wisdom, and success from his father, David. His life was set on a course for greatness. But despite the prophecy of blessing and wisdom, he made compromises that allowed contradictions to creep into his life.

The Bible tells us that Solomon began associating with his foreign wives' gods. At first, he didn't directly worship these idols. He didn't bow down to them, but he did something just as dangerous: he financed the building of shrines for his wives' gods. Solomon didn't realize that this small compromise allowed the spirit of error to enter his kingdom. He was no longer safeguarding the altar of God that his father David had raised. Instead, he was enabling the things that would weaken his kingdom and disrupt the future of his descendants.

In many of your lives today, there are contradictory prophecies at work. You may have received promises from God and spoken words of greatness, yet you are facing fierce battles. These battles often come from corrupt altars that have been set up, knowingly or unknowingly, by previous generations. Solomon's downfall was directly linked to the altars his wives built for their foreign gods. Similarly, many of you are dealing with ancestral altars, spiritual attacks, and inherited struggles that contradict the blessings God has spoken over your life.

But here is the truth: prophecies can be corrected when destiny altars are repaired. The past does not limit God's deliverance; He can intervene to redirect your future. Even when contradictory forces seem to be gaining ground, the commanded blessing and commanded deliverance can overthrow those altars and establish God's original intent for your life.

Solomon's story serves as a warning to us all. He had the opportunity to fix the altar and return to the pure worship of God, but he ignored the warning signs. As a result, the spirit of error overtook him, and the kingdom was eventually torn away from his lineage. The prophet Ahijah had already prophesied to Jeroboam, Solomon's servant, that the kingdom would be divided because Solomon failed to uphold the covenant with God.

The lesson here is clear: never ignore the altar. The fire upon your altar must never go out. Many of you are experiencing battles in your career, relationships, and spiritual life because the altar in your life has been neglected or corrupted. You allow influences, whether people, habits, or distractions, to distract you from God. And yet, others are actively servicing their altars and aligning with God's purpose. You wonder why they seem to be flourishing while you struggle. The difference is the altar.

The altar you despise is the very thing that will determine your destiny. The altar you ignore is the gateway through which the enemy gains access. That is why it is essential to maintain a strong altar, a place of continuous communion with God. When your altar is alive, the enemy's arrows will have no power over you. Let them throw their attacks; they will be deflected 1,000 times over because your altar stands strong.

In 1 Kings 11, we see the consequence of Solomon's errors. Because he ignored the altar, the kingdom was taken from his family. However, because of David's faithful altar, God showed mercy. The kingdom wasn't fully torn away during Solomon's lifetime, and one tribe was left for the sake of David's covenant with God. But Jeroboam, the servant who received the prophecy, didn't escape the same fate. Even though he was allowed to reign, he, too, let the spirit of error pollute his reign, and his dynasty fell into the same trap of idolatry.

The spirit of error seeks to pollute destiny altars, opening the door for negative prophecies to come to pass. But as we stand in prayer and repentance, correct our altars, and command deliverance, God will reverse the curse. He will restore what has been stolen, and you will walk in the fullness of the commanded blessing.

Tonight, contradictory prophecies will be overturned as you align your altar with God's will. You may have been told that you would fail and wouldn't rise above certain limitations, but God's commanded blessing will bring deliverance. The same God who reversed the fate of Esther, placing her in a position of power and influence after Vashti was dethroned, is the same God who will reverse the course of your life. Esther didn't strive for the throne; God's commanded blessing placed her there. Similarly, there are divine shifts that God is preparing for you, and all you need to do is align with His altar.

I don't know who is trying to remove what God ordained for you. I don't know who is plotting against your breakthrough or your favor. But as you stand in faith tonight, God's altar will empower your altar, and those contradictory forces will fall. Vastly was banished, and Esther was crowned. Likewise, your enemies will be overthrown, and you will take your rightful place in God's kingdom.

The spirit of error will not prevail in your life. As you maintain your altar, as you uphold God's covenant, you will see His commanded blessing manifest in every area of your life. Let this be the moment of your breakthrough, where everything changes, and the majesty of God's deliverance is revealed in you. Amen.

CHAPTER THREE

THE INFLUENCE OF RELATIONSHIPS ON DESTINY

The relationships we form significantly impact the trajectory of our lives. This truth is evident in Solomon's life, whose choices in relationships determined not only his destiny but also that of his descendants. The Queen of Sheba offers us a glimpse of what a positive, destiny-affirming relationship looks like, while the other women Solomon married demonstrate how wrong alliances can dismantle a person's life and call.

1 Kings 10:1-3 TLB tells us that the Queen of Sheba visited Solomon not to lead him astray but to experience the presence of God manifesting through his life. She was drawn by the wisdom and blessings that surrounded Solomon and sought to benefit from the divine favor that rested upon him. This starkly contrasts the other women in Solomon's life, who worshiped foreign gods and gradually turned his heart away from the one true God.

Solomon married these women for peace. He thought he would secure harmony in his kingdom by forging alliances with them. But little did he know these relationships would turn his life into pieces. The peace he sought was not the peace of God but a temporary, superficial peace that came at the cost of his spiritual integrity. This is a powerful lesson for us: not every relationship we enter into brings peace from God. Although some relationships seem beneficial in the short term, they lead to long-term destruction.

The Queen of Sheba is a divine contrast to the other women Solomon encountered. Her motives were pure; she desired to discover the wisdom and presence of God in Solomon's life. She wasn't there to manipulate or to draw Solomon away from his faith. Instead, she sought the riches of God's wisdom. This is the type of relationship we should strive to form. Some people come into our lives because they recognize the presence of God at work in us, and they desire to benefit from and contribute to that divine purpose.

In life, there are times when God decides to rewrite a person's story. He appoints individuals who carry divine authority to influence and redirect the destinies of others. The Bible shows us that God sometimes works through seasons, using specific individuals for particular moments. However, there are also times when God establishes something permanent that will last beyond a season.

As far as I am concerned, God is no longer doing things seasonally; He's doing things permanently. The stream of blessings that has begun in this ministry is not seasonal; it is a permanent stream. The lessons from Solomon's life, however, remind us that even when God begins a permanent work, the relationships we form can either reinforce or jeopardize that work.

1 Kings 10:5 TLB speaks of what the Queen of Sheba observed when she visited Solomon. The Bible says she was overwhelmed by the wisdom, wealth, and honor surrounding him. Think about what her eyes captured. She didn't just see material wealth; she witnessed a manifestation of God's favor and blessings. Solomon's kingdom reflected his relationship with God at the time, a

reflection of the spiritual altar that David, his father, had left behind.

Your family altar is a crucial element in the outcome of your life. Just as Solomon benefited from the altar that David had maintained, so too can you experience blessings when the altars of your forefathers align with God. But if the altar is neglected, unserviced, or corrupted, it can become a gateway for negative prophecies to manifest.

Spiritual things are powerful. They are so potent that you may become a victim of those spiritual forces if you are not intentional about them. An unguarded spiritual life is an invitation for destruction. But when you intentionally cultivate a relationship with God, maintain your altar, and remain open to His guidance, you will soar like David. David was a man who knew the value of a living altar. He maintained a constant connection with God, which became a legacy that elevated Solomon.

The life of Solomon reflected the life of David. Solomon's wisdom, wealth, and favor directly resulted from the altar David had built during his lifetime. David had fought battles, repented of his sins, and remained steadfast in his devotion to God. That devotion was passed down to Solomon, who began his reign on a foundation of glory. But the life of Rehoboam, Solomon's son, reflected Solomon's altar. By the time Solomon died, his heart had turned away from God, and the altar that had once been a source of blessing became corrupted. The consequences of that shift were felt in Rehoboam's reign.

Unlike his father's, Solomon's altar did not add or elevate his son. Instead, it eliminated the favor and blessings that should have been Rehoboam's inheritance. Solomon was no longer alive when the negative prophecy about the division of his kingdom came to pass, but Rehoboam had the opportunity to reverse the situation. However, he failed to do so. In 1 Kings 12:6-9, we see how Rehoboam rejected the wise counsel of the elders and chose to follow the foolish advice of his peers. This decision, rooted in pride and arrogance, fulfilled the negative prophecy, and the kingdom was torn apart.

There is a profound lesson here: relationships matter, both the ones we inherit and the ones we choose. David's relationship with God elevated Solomon, but Solomon's relationship with his foreign wives led to the downfall of his lineage. Rehoboam could have chosen to rebuild the altar and return to the ways of his grandfather, David, but he didn't. Instead, he allowed the corruption of his father's relationships to dictate his future.

God can bless you with favor, honor, strength, and courage, just as He blessed Solomon. But the relationships you form will either enhance or hinder those blessings. In Solomon's case, God blessed him with wisdom, wealth, and power. The intriguing aspect of this blessing was that it wasn't the material things that attracted the Queen of Sheba. It was the level of wisdom Solomon operated in. She marveled at the wisdom that came from his relationship with God, a wisdom that was a direct result of the altar David had maintained.

This should make us pause and reflect on our own lives. What kind of relationships are we forming? Are we allowing people into our lives who will turn us away from God, or are we aligning ourselves with those who recognize and respect the presence of God in us? The Queen of Sheba didn't come to Solomon to lead him astray; she came because she wanted to experience the presence of God in his life. However, the foreign women Solomon married had no interest in his relationship with God; they were only interested in leading him to worship their idols.

The relationships we nurture can either propel or derail us toward our destiny. When you align yourself with people who respect and honor God's presence in your life, your destiny will unfold in ways you never imagined. But when you form relationships with those without regard for your spiritual life, you may find yourself straying from God's path.

David's life was a testimony of what it means to maintain a living altar. He wasn't perfect but intentional about his relationship with God. And because of that intentionality, he left a legacy of blessing that elevated his son Solomon. But Solomon didn't maintain that same level of devotion, so the blessings he inherited didn't carry over to his son Rehoboam.

In conclusion, relationships have the power to affect destiny. Whether it is the relationships you form in your lifetime or the relationships that come as part of your heritage, they all shape your future. Solomon's life teaches us that even a man blessed with wisdom, wealth, and favor can fall if he forms the wrong alliances. But it also shows us that when we align ourselves with people like the Queen of Sheba, who seek the presence of God, we are positioned to walk in the fullness of our destiny.

The Desperation For The Blessing: A Gateway To Thriving And Sustenance

The blessing of God is not a mere wish or good fortune; it is a divine force that empowers a person to thrive, succeed, and overcome all odds. Throughout the Bible, we see men and women who became desperate for this blessing, recognizing that life's adversities would have the final say without it. The blessing is the power that prepares you for the challenges of life. It is a shield against adversity, a force that ensures that you will emerge victorious no matter what you face.

When we speak of being desperate for the blessing, we are not talking about desperation in the negative sense. It is the kind of desperation that Jacob displayed when he wrestled with God. It is a holy pursuit, a recognition that without the blessing, life will not unfold as intended. Jacob understood this when he declared, "I will not let you go unless you bless me" (Genesis 32:26). He knew that without God's blessing, he could not move forward in his journey.

The word "blessed" carries a significant meaning. It speaks of the power to thrive and succeed despite your obstacles. The blessing of God turns a man into a powerhouse. When God's blessing rests upon you, it transforms every area of your life. The invisible force works behind the scenes, ensuring that what would destroy others cannot kill you. It doesn't mean you won't face challenges; the challenges will not have the final say.

To be blessed is to carry within you the power to multiply, increase, and sustain what God has given you. This is why the blessing is the key to proliferation and sustenance. You can acquire things without the blessing but will struggle to keep them. With the blessing, you are empowered to develop, maintain, and expand.

Consider the life of Abraham. God's blessing on him didn't just bring material wealth; it ensured that his descendants would inherit a legacy that stretched far beyond his lifetime. The blessing wasn't temporary; it was generational. It passed from Abraham to Isaac and from Isaac to Jacob. This is what it means to be desperate for the blessing; it is to recognize that what you are seeking is not just for yourself but for those who will come after you. The blessing is the seed that ensures generational impact.

Now, let us explore the five blessings that play a crucial role in our lives. When understood and sought after with the right heart, these blessings become the foundation upon which we build our lives.

The Blessing Of Your Biological Parents

The first and most foundational blessing is the blessing of your biological parents. This blessing is not to be taken lightly. Many people overlook the significance of parental blessings, but in the spiritual realm, the words of a parent carry tremendous weight. The Bible is clear on this. Exodus 20:12 says, "Honor your father and your mother, that your days may be long in the land that the Lord your God is giving you." The honor that children give to their parents unlocks a blessing that leads to long life and prosperity.

There is something powerful about the blessing of a parent. When a father or mother says a word of blessing over their child, they release a spiritual covering. This covering shields the child from many of life's adversities. It is the foundation upon which the child's future is built. Isaac blessed Jacob, which became the key to Jacob's future. Even though Jacob had to flee from his brother Esau, the blessing remained with him. No matter where he went, the blessing followed.

A parent's blessing is not just a formality. It is a spiritual transaction. When parents bless their children, they invoke God's favor and protection. Even in cultures and traditions worldwide, the importance of parental blessings is recognized. In many African cultures, for instance, parents are regarded as the gatekeepers of their children's future. A child who dishonors their parents risks missing out on this crucial blessing.

Consider the story of Joseph. Despite being sold into slavery by his brothers, his father Jacob's blessing remained upon him. Joseph thrived even in a foreign land because the blessing had been spoken over him. When his brothers came to Egypt for food, they were unaware that the brother they had betrayed was now a powerful ruler. This is the power of parental blessings; they sustain you even when life throws unexpected challenges your way.

However, the blessing of parents is not automatic. It requires a heart of honor. Children must honor their parents not just with words but with actions. Honor opens the door for the blessing to flow. Many people today have blocked the flow of their blessings because of dishonor. They speak ill of their parents, disobey their instructions, and treat them contemptuously. But when you honor your parents, you position yourself to receive the full measure of their blessing.

There is also the reverse: when parents speak negative words to their children, those words can become a curse. This is why parents need to be mindful of the words they speak. A father's angry outburst or a mother's careless words can plant seeds of destruction in a child's life. Parents must learn to speak blessings, even in difficult situations. Words have power, and the words of a parent carry even more weight.

In the case of Isaac and Jacob, we see how a father's blessing can set the course of a child's future. Isaac blessed Jacob, believing he was blessing Esau, but the blessing took effect regardless of who received it. This shows us that a blessing cannot be taken back once a blessing is spoken. It is a spiritual decree that carries authority. Even when Esau begged his father for a blessing, Isaac could not reverse what he had already spoken over Jacob.

As a parent, you must understand the power you hold in shaping your child's destiny. Your words can either build them up or tear them down. Be intentional about blessing your children. Speak life into them, declare God's favor over them, and watch as those blessings manifest in their lives.

For those who may not have received the blessing of their biological parents, it is essential to remember that God can restore what was lost. You can still receive the blessing of God, which supersedes all other blessings. God is a father to the fatherless, and His blessing can break every curse and rewrite your story. Even if your earthly parents have not blessed you, the blessing of God is available to you through Christ.

The story of Jabez in 1 Chronicles 4:9-10 is a powerful example of this. Jabez was born into a family where his mother named him "Pain" because of the circumstances surrounding his birth. But

Jabez refused to accept that identity. He cried out to God, asking for a blessing, and God granted his request. This shows us that even if we do not receive the blessing of our biological parents, we can still cry out to God for His blessing.

Lastly, the blessing of your biological parents is a powerful force that can shape your life. It is a blessing that should be sought after with honor and respect. But even if that blessing is not available, the blessing of God is always within reach. Be desperate for the blessing, whether it comes from your parents or directly from God. It is the key to thriving, succeeding against all odds, and sustaining the blessings that God has given you.

The Blessing Of The Poor, Widows, Orphans, And The Less Privileged

Caring for the poor, widows, orphans, and the less privileged brings a great and often overlooked dimension of blessing. This blessing is not only a divine mandate but also an avenue through which God's favor flows into the giver's life. Job understood this principle, and his life exemplified the rewards of showing kindness to those in need.

In Job 29:13-18, Job recounts how he had received the blessing of those he had helped:

"The blessing of a perishing man came upon me, and I caused the widow's heart to sing for joy. I put on righteousness, which clothed me; my justice was like a robe and a turban. I was eyes to the blind and feet to the lame. I was a father to the poor, and I searched out the case I did not know."

Job's account reflects the heart of someone who deeply understood the importance of extending compassion and care to society's most vulnerable. His acts of kindness were not just social obligations; they were spiritual investments that brought about a profound sense of blessing and favor in his life. Job's righteousness was not measured only by his piety but by his actions toward those who had no one else to rely on.

The blessing of the poor, the widows, the orphans, and the less privileged is a different kind of blessing. It is a blessing that carries a deep sense of fulfillment and divine favor. When you touch the lives of those who cannot repay you, you feel the heart of God. The Bible is filled with promises of blessings for those who look after the less fortunate. Proverbs 19:17 says, "Whoever is generous to the poor lends to the Lord, and He will repay him for his deed." This is not just a moral principle; it is a spiritual law that operates in the realm of divine favor.

When we care for the poor and the marginalized, we align ourselves with God's heart. God defends the weak, and His blessing rests upon those who do the same. The Bible speaks repeatedly about the importance of caring for widows and orphans. In James 1:27, we are told that "pure and undefiled religion before God the Father is this: to visit orphans and widows in their trouble, and to keep oneself unspotted from the world." Caring for those in need is not optional in our walk with God—it is central to our faith.

The Power Of Compassion In Unlocking Blessings

Compassion is a force that moves the heart of God. When we show compassion to the poor, we are not just doing a good deed but participating in God's work. Jesus Himself said in Matthew 25:40, "Since you did it to one of the least of these, My brethren, you did it to Me." Every act of kindness we extend to those in need is an act of service to God. This is why there is such a powerful blessing attached to it.

The blessing of the poor, widows, orphans, and the less privileged operates in a way that transcends human understanding. You may not receive material wealth in return for your kindness, but you will experience God's favor in ways that cannot be quantified. Peace comes from knowing you have been a vessel of God's love to someone in need. A joy comes from seeing the smile on the face of a widow who has been helped or the relief in the eyes of an orphan who has been cared for.

Consider the story of Ruth and Boaz. Boaz was a man of great wealth and influence, but his kindness to Ruth, a poor widow, set him apart. Boaz went beyond what was required by the law and showed extraordinary generosity to Ruth. In return, Boaz received the blessing of a godly wife and became part of the lineage of Jesus Christ. The blessing upon Boaz was far greater than anything he could have imagined. This is the power of showing kindness to those in need; the blessing it brings is not just for this life but for future generations.

The Reward Of Giving To The Less Privileged

Giving to the less privileged brings a reward, but it is not always visible to the human eye. Sometimes, the reward comes as divine protection; other times, it is an unexpected favor or breakthrough. Job experienced this in his life. He was known as a man who cared deeply for the poor and the suffering, and this compassion was one of the reasons for the favor and blessings that flowed in his life.

In Job 29:16, he says, "I was a father to the needy, and I searched out the case that I did not know." This shows us that Job didn't just wait for people to come to him for help; he actively sought out those in need. This is the kind of heart that God blesses. Job's service to the poor brought him divine favor, and even though he went through trials, God restored him and blessed him even more abundantly.

The reward of giving is not always immediate, but it is sure. The

Bible tells us in Luke 6:38, “Give, and it will be given to you: good measure, pressed down, shaken together, and running over will be put into your bosom. With the same measure you use, it will be measured back to you.” When you give to the less privileged, you are planting seeds that will produce a harvest in your life. These seeds may take time to grow, but when they do, they make a blessing far more significant than what you gave.

God's Heart For The Poor And Vulnerable

God’s heart is incredibly tender toward the poor, the widows, the orphans, and the less privileged. Throughout the Bible, we see God’s concern for the marginalized and His call for His people to care for them. Deuteronomy 10:18 says, “He defends the cause of the fatherless and the widow, and loves the foreigner residing among you, giving them food and clothing.” This is the heart of God; He is the defender of the weak, and He calls us to be His hands and feet in the world.

When we take care of the poor, we are not just fulfilling a social obligation; we are participating in God's work. We are joining Him in His mission to bring justice and compassion to the world. This is why there is such a powerful blessing attached to caring for the less privileged; it is a reflection of God’s own heart. We position ourselves to receive His favor when we align ourselves with His purposes.

It is important to remember that caring for people experiencing poverty is not just about giving money. While financial support is essential, many other ways to bless the less privileged exist. We can provide our time, talents, and resources to help those in need. We can offer a listening ear, a helping hand, or a word of encouragement. The key is to be intentional about looking for ways to serve those who are vulnerable.

Living A Life Of Generosity

Generosity is the key to unlocking the blessings of the poor, the widows, the orphans, and the less privileged. When we live a life of generosity, we position ourselves to receive God's favor in ways we cannot imagine. The Bible tells us in Proverbs 11:25, "A generous person will prosper; whoever refreshes others will be refreshed." This spiritual principle applies to every area of life. When we refresh others, God refreshes us.

Living a life of generosity means looking for opportunities to bless others, being intentional about caring for the less fortunate, going beyond the bare minimum, and seeking to make a difference in the lives of others. When we live this way, we attract God's blessings into our own lives.

In summary, blessing the poor, widows, orphans, and less privileged is a powerful and transformative blessing. It carries with it God's favor and the joy of knowing that we are participating in His work. When we show kindness to those in need, we position ourselves to receive blessings beyond what we see. Let us be desperate for this kind of blessing, which is the key to a life of favor, fulfillment, and divine reward.

The Blessing Of Your Family

Family is one of the most fundamental structures that God has designed for humanity. We often receive some of our greatest blessings through the family. The blessing of your family is a unique and powerful form of favor that has the potential to shape destinies, secure futures, and bring about fulfillment in ways that extend beyond individual achievements. Proverbs 31:28 says, "Her children rise and call her blessed; her husband also, and he praises her." This verse captures the essence of family blessings, honor, respect, and love given and received within the family unit.

The blessing that flows from your family can sustain you through life's journey. It is the kind of blessing that provides support, encouragement, and strength in difficult times. The power of family cannot be underestimated, for it is often within the family that our foundational values are established and nurtured. When a family is blessed, that blessing does not remain contained within the family; it spills over into every area of life, bringing favor, success, and peace.

The Foundation Of Family Blessings

The foundation of family blessings is built on relationships. The relationship between parents and children, siblings, and spouses forms the core of this blessing. Each family member has a role in creating an environment where blessings can flow. Proverbs 31:28 emphasizes the role of children and spouses in honoring one another, and this honor is a critical ingredient in unlocking the family's blessing. When children rise and call their parents blessed, they acknowledge the sacrifices, love, and care poured into their lives. This act of recognition is a powerful blessing that reinforces the bonds within the family.

The same is true for spouses. A husband who praises his wife shows appreciation for her efforts and affirms her value within the family. This creates a cycle of blessing where each family member feels valued, respected, and honored. When honor is present, blessings flow freely. This is why the Bible places so much emphasis on the family unit. In Ephesians 6:1-3, children are instructed to honor their parents, with the promise that it will go well with them and they will enjoy a long life on the earth. This is a direct link between family honor and the blessings that follow.

The Role Of Parents In Bestowing Blessings

Parents play a significant role in bestowing blessings upon their children. Throughout Scripture, we see examples of parents speaking blessings over their offspring. In the Old Testament, it was common for fathers to pronounce blessings over their children before their death, and these blessings carried great significance. In Genesis 27, we see Isaac blessing his son Jacob, which shaped Jacob's life. Even though the blessing was given under unusual circumstances, it profoundly impacted Jacob's destiny. This shows us that the words spoken by parents can shape their children's future.

When parents bless their children, they speak life, favor, and prosperity into their lives. This is not just a cultural or religious tradition; it is a spiritual principle that has the power to unlock divine favor. Proverbs 18:21 says, "Death and life are in the power of the tongue." When parents use their words to bless their children, they plant the seeds of success, favor, and protection that will bear fruit in time. Parents must intentionally speak blessings over their children, for those words carry weight in the spiritual realm.

At the same time, parents are also responsible for creating an environment where blessings can thrive. This means nurturing their children, providing guidance, and modeling godly behavior. The Bible instructs parents to "train up a child in the way he should go, and when he is old, he will not depart from it" (Proverbs 22:6). This training is a form of blessing in itself, for it lays the foundation for a life of purpose, integrity, and success. Parents who invest in their children's spiritual, emotional, and intellectual development are positioning them to receive God's blessing.

The Role Of Children In Honoring Their Parents

Just as parents are responsible for blessing their children, children also have a role to play in honoring their parents. Honor is a critical component of family blessings. When children honor their parents, they are fulfilling a biblical commandment and positioning themselves to receive blessings. In Exodus 20:12, we are commanded to "honor your father and your mother, that your days may be long upon the land which the Lord your God is giving you." This promise of long life and prosperity is tied directly to honoring one's parents.

Honor is more than obedience; it is about showing respect, love, and appreciation for the role that parents have played in shaping their children's lives. When children rise and call their parents blessed, as Proverbs 31:28 suggests, they acknowledge the sacrifices, wisdom, and love their parents have invested in them. This acknowledgment is a form of blessing that strengthens the family bond and invites God's favor.

In many cultures, honoring one's parents extends beyond childhood. Even as adults, we are called to continue honoring our parents through respect, care, and support. This ongoing honor maintains the flow of blessings within the family. When adult children honor their elderly parents by providing or caring for them in their later years, they fulfill a biblical mandate that brings continued blessings.

The Power Of Unity In The Family

One of the most powerful aspects of family blessings is its unity. Psalm 133:1 says, "Behold, how good and how pleasant it is for brethren to dwell together in unity!" Unity within the family creates an atmosphere where blessings can flow freely. When family members are united in love, respect, and honor, they make a solid foundation to withstand life's challenges.

This unity does not mean that there will never be disagreements or conflicts. Every family faces challenges, but how those challenges are addressed makes the difference. A family that is committed to resolving disputes with grace and understanding is a family that will continue to experience blessings. The family's unity brings peace, a critical ingredient in a blessed life. Proverbs 17:1 says, “Better is a dry morsel with quietness than a house full of feasting with strife.” Peace within the family is far more valuable than material wealth or success.

When a family is united, it also reflects the unity of the Trinity: Father, Son, and Holy Spirit. God’s design for family is rooted in unity, and when we embrace that design, we align ourselves with His purposes. This alignment allows blessings to flow into every area of our lives. A family that prays together works together and supports one another will experience the fullness of God’s blessings in ways that go beyond individual achievements.

The Impact Of Family Blessings On Future Generations

The blessing of the family does not end with the current generation. Family blessings have a lasting impact on future generations. Just as negative behaviors and patterns can be passed down through generations, so can blessings. When a family is blessed, that blessing often extends to children, grandchildren, and even great-grandchildren. This is why it is so essential to cultivate an environment of blessing within the family.

In 2 Timothy 1:5, Paul speaks of the faith passed down to Timothy from his grandmother, Lois, and his mother, Eunice. This is an example of how the blessing of faith can be passed down through generations. Timothy's spiritual heritage became the foundation for his own ministry. In the same way, the blessings we cultivate within our families can have a lasting impact on our descendants.

Not just spiritual blessings can be passed down; material blessings, wisdom, and favor can also be inherited by future generations. Proverbs 13:22 tells us that “a good man leaves an inheritance to his children’s children.” This inheritance goes beyond financial wealth—it includes the legacy of character, integrity, and godliness that we leave behind. When we live in such a way that our family is blessed, we create a legacy that will benefit future generations.

What am I saying? The blessing of the family is a powerful and transformative force. It comes from the relationships, unity, and honor that exist within the family unit. Parents are responsible for blessing their children, and children are called to honor their parents. When these principles are implemented, the family becomes a source of strength, support, and divine favor.

Family blessings have the power to shape destinies, secure futures, and create a lasting impact on future generations. By nurturing relationships, promoting unity, and embracing the biblical principles of honor and respect, we position ourselves and our families to experience the fullness of God's blessings. Let us value and cherish the blessing of family, for it is one of the greatest gifts that God has given to us.

The Blessing Of Your Spiritual Father

The blessing of a spiritual father is another of the most profound and life-changing blessings an individual can receive. This blessing goes beyond the natural and taps into the spiritual realm, where divine favor and grace flow freely. When your spiritual father invokes a blessing upon you, that blessing can change your life, open doors, and secure your future. This blessing stays with you, shaping your path and destiny in ways that can only be understood through spiritual discernment.

Throughout Scripture, we see the importance of spiritual fathers and their role in blessing their spiritual children. From Elijah and Elisha to Paul and Timothy, the concept of spiritual fatherhood has been central to the development of individuals in the kingdom of God. The blessing from a spiritual father is not just a verbal proclamation but a spiritual impartation that carries the weight of authority, anointing, and divine favor.

The Significance Of Spiritual Fathers

A spiritual father has been placed in your life to guide, mentor, and nurture your spiritual growth. They are not just pastors or leaders; they have been given spiritual authority to speak into your life and help you navigate the complexities of your spiritual journey. The relationship between a spiritual father and their spiritual children is deeply rooted in honor, submission, and respect. When you recognize and honor your spiritual father, you open up to receive the blessings flowing from that relationship.

In 1 Corinthians 4:15, Apostle Paul speaks of his role as a spiritual father to the Corinthians, saying, "For though you might have ten thousand instructors in Christ, yet you do not have many fathers; for in Christ Jesus I have begotten you through the gospel." This distinction between instructors and fathers is significant. Instructors can teach and impart knowledge, but fathers go beyond teaching; they nurture, correct, and bless their spiritual children. The blessing of a spiritual father directly results from the relationship cultivated between them and their spiritual children.

When a spiritual father invokes a blessing upon you, it is not just a formality or a ritual. It is a spiritual transaction that takes place in the heavenly realms. The blessing spoken over you carries the weight of authority and anointing your spiritual father has received from God. This is why it is essential to honor and respect your spiritual father, for the blessing they speak over you is not just their own; it comes from God.

The Power Of Spiritual Authority

One of the reasons why the blessing of a spiritual father is so powerful is because it is rooted in spiritual authority. Spiritual authority is the divine right to command, direct, and influence in the spiritual realm. When your spiritual father speaks a blessing over you, you are exercising the spiritual authority entrusted to them by God. This authority is not taken lightly, and it is not something that can be exercised without the leading of the Holy Spirit.

In the Bible, we see numerous examples of spiritual fathers exercising their authority to bless their spiritual children. One such example is found in the relationship between Elijah and Elisha. In 2 Kings 2, we see the moment when Elijah is about to be taken to heaven, and Elisha asks for a double portion of Elijah's spirit. Elijah responds by saying, "You have asked a hard thing. Nevertheless, if you see me when I am taken from you, it shall be so for you; but if not, it shall not be so" (2 Kings 2:10). This interaction highlights the spiritual authority that Elijah had over Elisha. The blessing that Elisha received was not just a result of his request; it was the result of Elijah's spiritual authority and the relationship cultivated between them.

When your spiritual father blesses you, they are not just speaking words; they are exercising the spiritual authority God gave them. This authority carries weight in the spiritual realm, and it can change circumstances, open doors, and release divine favor into your life. The blessing of a spiritual father is not something to be taken lightly, for it carries the power and authority of heaven.

The Role Of Submission In Receiving The Blessing

One fundamental principle in receiving the blessing of your spiritual father is submission. Submission is not about control or manipulation; it is about recognizing and honoring the authority that God has placed in your life. When you submit to your spiritual father, you are positioning yourself to receive God's full blessing for you. Submission is an act of humility and trust and is a critical component in receiving spiritual blessings.

In Hebrews 13:17, we are instructed to "obey those who rule over you, and be submissive, for they watch out for your souls, as those who must give account. Let them do so with joy and not grief, for that would be unprofitable for you." This verse signifies spiritual fathers' responsibility to watch over their spiritual children's souls. It also emphasizes the importance of submission in the relationship between spiritual fathers and their children. When you submit to your spiritual father's authority, you acknowledge that they have been placed in your life by God to guide, protect, and bless you.

Submission is not always easy, especially in a culture that often values independence and self-reliance. However, submission is a key to unlocking blessings in the kingdom of God. When you submit to your spiritual father, you align yourself with the order and structure that God established in the spiritual realm. This alignment opens the door for the blessings of heaven to flow into your life.

The Blessing That Stays

One of the unique aspects of the blessing of a spiritual father is that it stays with you. This is not a temporary blessing that fades with time; it is a lasting impartation that works in your life long after it has been spoken. A spiritual father's blessing carries a permanence rooted in the authority and anointing of the one who says it. When your spiritual father blesses you, that blessing becomes a part of your spiritual inheritance and continues to bear fruit throughout your life.

In Genesis 48, we see the moment when Jacob, as a spiritual father, blesses Joseph's sons, Ephraim and Manasseh. Even though Jacob was nearing the end of his life, the blessing he spoke over his grandsons had a lasting impact. The blessing did not fade with

Jacob's death; it remained with Ephraim and Manasseh, shaping their destinies and the destinies of their descendants. This is the power of a spiritual father's blessing—it stays.

When your spiritual father blesses you, they are not just discussing your current situation. They are speaking into your future, your destiny, and the generations that will come after you. The blessing of a spiritual father is like a seed planted in your life's soil. Over time, that seed will grow and bear fruit, producing a harvest of favor, success, and divine provision.

The Impact Of Spiritual Blessings On Your Destiny

The blessing of your spiritual father has a direct impact on your destiny. It has the power to unlock previously closed doors, bring breakthroughs in areas where you have struggled, and position you for divine assignments that are part of God's plan for your life. The blessing of a spiritual father is not just about personal success; it is about aligning yourself with God's purpose for your life.

In the Bible, we repeatedly see the impact of spiritual blessings on individuals' destinies. When Elijah blessed Elisha with a double portion of his spirit, it positioned Elisha to carry on the prophetic ministry and perform even greater miracles than Elijah had. When Paul blessed Timothy and laid hands on him, imparting spiritual gifts, Timothy became an influential leader in the early church. These blessings were not just about the individuals but about fulfilling God's plan for their lives.

When your spiritual father blesses you, they are not just speaking to your current circumstances; they are talking to your destiny. A spiritual father's blessing can shape your future and align you with God's purpose for your life. It is a blessing that carries divine favor, provision, and protection, ensuring you are equipped for the journey ahead.

Honoring Your Spiritual Father

One of the most important aspects of receiving the blessing of your spiritual father is the principle of honor. Honor is the key that unlocks the blessing. When you honor your spiritual father, you are acknowledging the role they play in your life and the authority they carry. Honor is not just about words but about actions, attitude, and heart posture. When you honor your spiritual father, you create an atmosphere where blessings can flow freely.

In 1 Timothy 5:17, we are instructed to "*let the elders who rule well be counted worthy of double honor, especially those who labor in the word and doctrine.*" This principle of double honor is fundamental when it comes to spiritual fathers. The labor they undertake on behalf of their spiritual children is not just physical but spiritual. They watch over your soul, intercede for you in prayer, and seek God's will for your life. Honoring them is not just a matter of respect but a spiritual principle that positions you to receive their blessing.

When you honor your spiritual father, you also honor the God who placed them in your life. Spiritual fathers are not self-appointed; God chooses them to fulfill a specific role in your life. By honoring them, you recognize the divine order God established in the kingdom. This recognition opens the door for blessings to flow into your life.

The blessing of your spiritual father is a powerful gift that can shape your destiny, unlock divine favor, and secure your future. It stays with you, continuing to work in your life long after it has been spoken. When your spiritual father invokes a blessing upon you, it is not just a formality; it is a spiritual impartation that carries the weight of authority and divine favor.

The Blessing Of The Lord: The Ultimate Blessing

The blessing of the Lord is the ultimate blessing that a person can receive. Unlike other types of blessings, which may come from parents, spiritual fathers, or even the less privileged, the blessing of the Lord comes directly from God Himself. It is a blessing that encompasses every aspect of your life: spiritual, physical, emotional, and relational. When the blessing of the Lord is upon you, it begins to shape your destiny, open doors, and reconcile things that were broken in your life. It is a blessing that gives you another opportunity to fix your wrongs and make things right.

The Bible clarifies that the Lord's blessing is a powerful force that can transform a person's life. Proverbs 10:22 says, "The blessing of the Lord makes one rich, and He adds no sorrow with it." This verse highlights the completeness of God's blessing. It is not just about material wealth or success; it is about experiencing the fullness of life without the burdens or sorrows that often come with worldly achievements. When the blessing of the Lord shows up in your life, it brings peace, joy, fulfillment, and divine protection. It lifts you above challenges and positions you to walk in the favor and purpose of God.

The Power Of Reconciliation And Restoration

One aspect of the Lord's blessing is its ability to reconcile and restore. Throughout the Bible, we see how God's blessing brings about reconciliation between people and God, between families, and even between individuals and their destinies. When God blesses someone, He doesn't just provide for their immediate needs; He restores broken relationships, mends shattered lives and reconnects people to their original purpose.

In the story of the prodigal son (Luke 15:11-32), we see a powerful example of the blessing of reconciliation. After squandering his inheritance and falling into poverty and shame, the prodigal son returns to his father. What he experiences upon his return is a perfect example of the blessing of the Lord. Instead of being rejected or condemned, he is welcomed back with open arms. His father restores him to his rightful place in the family, not as a servant but as a son. This act of reconciliation is a powerful demonstration of how God's blessing works to restore what was lost and fix what was broken.

The blessing of the Lord often brings about this kind of reconciliation in our lives. Whether reconciling us to God through forgiveness and grace or mending broken relationships with loved ones, the blessing of the Lord creates opportunities for restoration. It gives us another chance to make things right, to heal wounds, and to move forward in a way that aligns with God's plan for our lives.

The Blessing That Fixes Our Wrongs

Another key aspect of the Lord's blessing is its ability to give us another opportunity to fix our wrongs. We all make mistakes, and there are times in life when our wrong decisions or actions create barriers between us and the blessings God has for us. But the beauty of God's blessing is that it doesn't leave us in our mistakes. Instead, it gives us the grace and the opportunity to correct our wrongs and move forward.

One of the best examples is in the life of Peter, one of Jesus' disciples. After Peter denied Jesus three times, he was filled with guilt and shame. He had made a grave mistake, and his relationship with Jesus seemed broken beyond repair. But after Jesus' resurrection, He appeared to Peter, giving him another opportunity to reaffirm his love and commitment. In John 21:15-17, Jesus asks Peter three times, "Do you love Me?" This interaction was a moment of reconciliation and restoration. Jesus gave Peter the chance to fix his wrongs, be restored, and step into the purpose God had for him.

This is what the blessing of the Lord does in our lives. It doesn't allow us to stay stuck in our mistakes or failures. Instead, it creates a path for us to make things right, to be reconciled, and to move forward with a renewed sense of purpose. When God blesses you, He gives you the grace to fix the broken things in your life, whether broken relationships, missed opportunities, or personal failures. His blessing provides the strength and the opportunity to move forward in His will.

The Blessing That Makes You

The blessing of the Lord doesn't just reconcile and restore; it also makes you. It shapes you into the person God has called you to be and equips you with the resources, wisdom, and favor you need to fulfill your purpose. When God's blessing is upon your life, it begins to mold and refine you, preparing you for the challenges and opportunities.

In the story of Joseph, we see how the blessing of the Lord made him into the leader he was destined to be. Despite being sold into slavery by his brothers, falsely accused, and thrown into prison, Joseph remained under the blessing of the Lord. Genesis 39:2 says, "The Lord was with Joseph, and he was a successful man, and he was in the house of his master the Egyptian." Despite adversity, God's blessing was at work in Joseph's life, shaping him and preparing him for the day when he would become second-in-command over all of Egypt.

The blessing of the Lord does the same for us. It doesn't mean that we won't face challenges or hardships. But it does mean that even in difficult seasons, God's blessing is at work, shaping, refining, and preparing us for the future He has planned. The blessing of the Lord makes us into people of character, wisdom, and strength. It equips us to handle the responsibilities and opportunities of walking in God's purpose.

The Blessing That Opens Doors

The blessing of the Lord not only makes you, but it also opens doors that no man can shut. When God blesses you, His favor goes before you, creating opportunities and making a way where there seems to be no way. Throughout Scripture, we see how the blessing of the Lord opened doors for His people, leading them into places of influence, success, and victory.

In the book of Esther, we see how God's blessing opened doors for Esther to become queen and ultimately save her people from destruction. Despite the odds being stacked against her, Esther found favor in the eyes of the king. This favor was not just a result of her beauty or charm; it was the blessing of the Lord at work in her life, positioning her for a divine assignment. The blessing of the Lord opened doors for Esther that she could never have opened on her own.

In our own lives, the blessing of the Lord works in much the same way. It opens doors that we could never open on our own. It creates opportunities for advancement, success, and influence beyond our natural abilities or qualifications. When God's blessing is upon you, doors that were once closed begin to open, and you find yourself walking into places of favor and opportunity that only God could have orchestrated.

The Ultimate Source Of Provision

The blessing of the Lord is also the ultimate source of provision. When God blesses you, He provides for your needs in ways that go beyond natural means. Whether it's financial provision, physical healing, or emotional support, God's blessing ensures you have everything you need to fulfill His purpose for your life.

In the story of the Israelites in the wilderness, we see how God's blessing provided for their every need. The Israelites wandered in the desert for forty years, yet they lacked nothing. Deuteronomy 8:4 says, "Your garments did not wear out on you, nor did your foot swell these forty years." God's blessing sustained them, providing manna from heaven, water from a rock, and protection from enemies. Even in the most challenging and barren circumstances, God's blessing was the source of their provision.

In the same way, the blessing of the Lord provides for us today. It may not always come in the way we expect, but God's blessing ensures we have what we need to fulfill His will. Whether it's financial resources, divine connections, or supernatural wisdom, the blessing of the Lord provides for our every need.

Walking In The Blessing Of The Lord

The blessing of the Lord is available to all who walk in obedience to Him. While God's grace is freely given, His blessings often flow through our willingness to align ourselves with His will and His ways. Obedience, faith, and trust are key components in positioning ourselves to receive the full blessing of the Lord.

In Deuteronomy 28, we see a clear outline of the blessings of walking in obedience to God. The chapter begins with these words: "Now it shall come to pass, if you diligently obey the voice of the Lord your God, to observe all His commandments which I command you today, that the Lord your God will set you high above all nations of the earth. And all these blessings shall come upon you and overtake you because you obey the voice of the Lord your God" (Deuteronomy 28:1-2). The passage goes on to list the many blessings that come with obedience, blessings of provision, protection, favor, and success.

Walking in the blessing of the Lord requires us to remain connected to Him, seek His guidance, and live according to His Word. It is not about perfection but about a heart that is surrendered to God and willing to follow His leading. When we walk in obedience to God, His blessings begin to flow in every area of our lives.

The blessing of the Lord is the ultimate blessing, one that encompasses every aspect of our lives. It reconciles, restores, and allows us to fix our wrongs. It makes us into the people God has called us to be, opens doors no man can shut, and provides for our every need. When we obey God, His blessing flows into our lives, shaping our destiny and positioning us for His purpose. Let us seek to walk in the blessing of the Lord, knowing that it is the key to living a life of abundance, favor, and divine fulfillment.

CHAPTER FOUR

YOUR RESPONSIBILITY

As we have seen that the blessing of the Lord is available to all who seek it, but it doesn't come automatically. There is a responsibility on our part to actively pursue the blessing of God. Like any treasure of great value, the blessing requires intentionality, desire, and effort. In other words, we must go for the blessing. This is not about striving in the flesh or trying to earn God's favor but about aligning ourselves with His principles, seeking His face, and being ready to receive the abundant life He promises.

One of the key lessons we learn from the Bible is that blessings often follow action. God's promises are available but require us to take steps of faith, obedience, and persistence. This principle is evident in the lives of biblical figures who received extraordinary blessings, and it applies to us today. If you want to experience the full measure of God's blessing in your life, you must take responsibility for going after it.

The Desire To Pursue The Blessing

The first step in seeking a blessing is cultivating a genuine desire for it. Blessings don't come to those who are passive or indifferent. They come to those who hunger and thirst for God's things. Jesus said in Matthew 5:6, "Blessed are those who hunger and thirst for righteousness, for they shall be filled." This powerful promise reveals a key truth: if you want God's blessing, you must deeply desire it.

Throughout the Bible, we see examples of people who passionately pursued the blessing of God. One of the most notable examples is Jacob. In Genesis 32:24-30, Jacob wrestled with an angel of God all night, refusing to let go until he received a blessing. His persistence paid off, and he was blessed with a new name and destiny. This story shows us the importance of burning desire for the blessing. Jacob was willing to wrestle, strive, and persevere because he understood the value of God's blessing.

In our own lives, we must develop this same kind of desire. It's not enough to casually wish for God's blessing; we must hunger for it. This hunger drives us to seek God with all our hearts, to spend time in His presence, and to obey His Word. It is a desire that fuels our pursuit of God's best for our lives.

Aligning Yourself With God's Principles

Going for the blessing also involves aligning yourself with the principles of God. Blessings are not random or arbitrary; they are often the result of living in accordance with God's ways. In Deuteronomy 28:1-2, God says, "If you fully obey the Lord your God and carefully follow all His commands I give you today, the Lord your God will set you high above all the nations on earth. All these blessings will come on you and accompany you if you obey the Lord your God."

This passage reveals that obedience is a critical component of receiving the blessing. God's blessings are tied to His principles, and when we align ourselves with those principles, we position ourselves to receive His favor. This is not about earning God's love or approval; it's about living in a way that invites His blessings into our lives. Just as the rain falls naturally on a well-prepared field, the blessings of God naturally flow into the lives of those who obey His Word.

Aligning yourself with God’s principles means making choices that honor Him. It means living a life of integrity, humility, and faithfulness. It means treating others with love and respect, generosity, and forgiveness. When we live in this way, we open ourselves up to the flow of God's blessings. Just as a farmer prepares the soil before planting seeds, we must prepare our lives to receive the harvest of blessings that God has in store for us.

Seeking God’s Presence

Another key responsibility in going for the blessing is seeking the presence of God. The blessing of the Lord is closely connected to His presence. Where God is, His blessings abound. This is why it is important to seek God’s presence above all else. If you seek the blessing without seeking the One who gives it, you will miss the true essence of what it means to be blessed.

King David understood this truth. In Psalm 16:11, he declared, “You will show me the path of life; in Your presence is fullness of joy; at Your right hand are pleasures always.” David knew that the real blessing was material wealth or success and being close to God. When we seek God’s presence, we experience His peace, joy, wisdom, and guidance. These are the true blessings that lead to a life of abundance and fulfillment.

Seeking God’s presence requires intentionality. It means spending time in prayer, worship, and the study of His Word. It means drawing near to Him with an open and humble heart. James 4:8 says, “Draw near to God, and He will draw near to you.” This is a promise that when we try to seek God, He will meet us with His presence and blessing.

Walking In Faith And Expectation

Faith is another vital component of going for the blessing. The Bible tells us that "without faith, it is impossible to please Him, for he who comes to God must believe that He is, and that He is a rewarder of those who diligently seek Him" (Hebrews 11:6). If we are to receive the blessing, we must walk in faith and expectation, believing that God is able and willing to bless us.

Abraham is often called the father of faith because he believed God's promises even when they seemed impossible. In Genesis 12:2, God promised Abraham, "I will make you a great nation; I will bless you and make your name great; and you shall be a blessing." Abraham believed this promise and acted in faith, leaving his home and following God into the unknown. His faith was rewarded with blessings beyond his wildest dreams.

Like Abraham, we must believe that God is a reward for those who seek Him. We must have faith that His blessings are available to us and that He can do exceedingly abundantly above all we can ask or think (Ephesians 3:20). This kind of faith empowers us to take bold steps toward the blessing, knowing that God is faithful to fulfill His promises.

Faith also involves trusting God's timing. Sometimes, the blessing doesn't come immediately. It may take days, months, or even years before we see the full manifestation of what God has promised. But faith allows us to wait patiently and confidently, knowing that God is working all things together for our good (Romans 8:28). As we continue to trust Him, we position ourselves to receive the blessing in His perfect timing.

Obedience To God's Instruction

Going for the blessing also requires obedience to God's specific instructions for your life. Just as God gave Noah detailed instructions on how to build the ark (Genesis 6:14-22), He often gives us particular directions that are key to unlocking His blessings. These instructions may come through His word, through prayer, or through wise counsel. When we obey God's instructions, we position ourselves to receive His blessings.

Obedience is not always easy, especially when God's instructions don't make sense to us or seem difficult to follow. But we must remember that God's ways are higher than our ways, and His thoughts are higher than our thoughts (Isaiah 55:9). He sees the bigger picture and knows what is best for us. When we trust Him enough to obey, even when challenging, we open the door to His blessings.

The story of Naaman, the commander of the Syrian army, is a powerful example of how obedience can lead to blessing. In 2 Kings 5:1-14, Naaman was instructed by the prophet Elisha to wash in the Jordan River seven times to heal his leprosy. At first, Naaman resisted, thinking that the instruction was too simple and beneath him. But when he finally obeyed, he was completely healed. His obedience unlocked the blessing of healing.

In our own lives, there may be times when God asks us to do things that seem small, insignificant, or even difficult. But in those moments, our obedience can unlock the blessing we have been waiting for. Whether forgiving someone who has wronged us, stepping out in faith to start a new venture, or simply spending more time in prayer, our obedience to God's instructions is often the key to receiving His blessing.

Persistence In Prayer

Prayer is another important aspect of going for the blessing. In Luke 18:1-8, Jesus tells the parable of the persistent widow, who kept coming to a judge with her plea for justice. Although the judge initially ignored her, he eventually granted her request because of her persistence. Jesus used this story to teach us the importance of persistent prayer. He said, "Will not God bring about justice for His chosen ones, who cry out to Him day and night? Will He keep putting them off? I tell you, He will see that they get justice, and quickly" (Luke 18:7-8).

Persistence in prayer is a key to receiving the blessing. There are times when the blessing doesn't come immediately, and we must continue to pray, to seek, and to knock until the door is opened (Matthew 7:7). This persistence demonstrates our faith and our trust in God's ability to provide. It shows that we are serious about going for the blessing and that we are willing to wait on God's timing.

In the story of Elijah on Mount Carmel - 1 Kings 18:41-45, we see a powerful example of persistent prayer. After a long drought, Elijah prayed for rain. He sent his servant to look for signs of rain, but there was nothing. Elijah continued to pray, sending his servant back seven times before a small cloud finally appeared on the horizon. Elijah's persistence in prayer brought the blessing of rain, and it teaches us the importance of not giving up when we pray.

Hope it's clear that going for the blessing is not a passive endeavor. It requires desire, faith, obedience, persistence, and a deep hunger for the things of God. We must be intentional about aligning ourselves with God's principles, seeking His presence, and following His instructions. We must be persistent in prayer, believing that God is a reward for those who diligently seek Him.

As we take these steps, we position ourselves to receive God's blessing in our lives. Just as Jacob wrestled with the angel and refused to let go until he was blessed, we must be determined to pursue God's blessing with all our hearts. When we do, we can trust that God will honor our pursuit, and His blessings will flow into every area of our lives.

Be Hungry For The Blessing

In pursuing God's blessing, one of the most important attributes we must develop is hunger. Hunger for the blessing is a deep, inner longing for more of God and His favor upon our lives. It is an intense desire that pushes us beyond routine into a passionate quest for the fullness of what God offers. When you are hungry for the blessing, you are not satisfied with where you are spiritually, emotionally, or even materially. You know there is more, and you are willing to go after it with everything you have.

Hunger is a driving force. It is what separates those who casually wish for God's blessings from those who relentlessly pursue them. The Bible is full of examples of people hungry for the blessing and went to great lengths to obtain it. Their hunger was the key that unlocked the door to extraordinary favor, provision, and breakthrough in their lives.

The Importance Of Hunger

Hunger is vital because it propels you to act. Without hunger, there is no real motivation to seek or strive for the blessing. Hunger creates a sense of urgency. It stirs up a longing for change, growth, and transformation. When you are spiritually hungry, you cannot remain in a place of complacency. Instead, you constantly seek ways to draw nearer to God and experience more of His blessings.

In the physical realm, hunger causes us to seek food to satisfy our needs. Likewise, spiritual hunger causes us to seek out God's blessings to fulfill our deepest desires. Just as our bodies need nourishment to thrive, our spirits need the blessings of God to experience true fulfillment. When spiritually hungry, you won't settle for anything less than God's best for your life.

Jesus emphasized the importance of spiritual hunger in His Sermon on the Mount. He said, "Blessed are those who hunger and thirst for righteousness, for they shall be filled" (Matthew 5:6).

This promise reveals that hunger is a prerequisite for being filled with God's blessings. If you want to experience the fullness of God's blessings, you must develop a hunger for righteousness, for His presence, and for His favor in every area of your life.

Examples Of Hunger In The Bible

Numerous examples in the Bible of individuals who demonstrated an intense hunger for God's blessings are found. Their stories serve as perfect lessons for us today, showing how God responds to those who hunger for more of Him.

One such example is the woman with the issue of blood, as described in Mark 5:25-34. This woman had been suffering for twelve years, but despite her condition, she had a deep hunger for healing. When she heard about Jesus, she didn't wait passively for Him to come to her. Instead, she pressed through the crowd and reached out to touch the hem of His garment, believing that even a tiny connection with Jesus would bring her healing. Her hunger for the blessing of healing pushed her beyond the limits of her physical pain and societal rejection. Jesus responded to her faith and hunger by healing her completely.

This story illustrates that hunger drives you to go beyond what is comfortable. The woman's hunger led her to take risks and break cultural norms because she was desperate for a touch from God. Likewise, our hunger for the blessing must push us to step out in faith, seek God with boldness, and press through any obstacles that stand in our way.

Another powerful example of hunger is the story of blind Bartimaeus in Mark 10:46-52. When Bartimaeus heard that Jesus was passing by, he cried, "Jesus, Son of David, have mercy on me!" Even when the crowd tried to silence him, his hunger for healing caused him to cry out even louder. His persistence got Jesus' attention, and Bartimaeus received his sight because he refused to let his opportunity for blessing pass by.

Bartimaeus' hunger is a lesson in perseverance. When you are hungry for the blessing, you don't give up easily. You keep seeking, asking, and knocking until the door is opened. This kind of spiritual hunger moves God's heart and brings about supernatural results.

Hunger And Faith Work Together

Hunger for the blessing is closely connected to faith. Hunger and faith work hand in hand. When you are hungry for God's blessing, it demonstrates that you believe in His ability to provide and trust in His promises. Faith is the substance of things hoped for and the evidence of things not seen (Hebrews 11:1), and hunger fuels that hope and expectation.

The more you hunger for the blessing, the more you exercise your faith. Hunger stirs up a belief that God can do exceedingly abundantly above all that we can ask or think (Ephesians 3:20). It compels us to move beyond our current circumstances and limitations and to reach out for the abundance that God has in store for us.

We see this connection between hunger and faith in the life of the Canaanite woman in Matthew 15:21-28. When she approached Jesus, asking Him to heal her daughter, He initially ignored her. But her hunger for the blessing of healing would not allow her to walk away empty-handed. Even when Jesus tested her faith by saying it wasn't right to take the children's bread and give it to the dogs, she humbly persisted, saying, "Even the dogs eat the crumbs that fall from their master's table."

Her hunger for the blessing was so great that she was willing to take even the most minor portion of God's favor. Jesus responded to her hunger and faith by granting her request and healing her daughter. Her story teaches us that hunger, when combined with faith, has the power to break through barriers and release God's blessings into our lives.

Hunger For God’s Presence

One of the greatest blessings we can ever receive is God's presence. Being hungry for the blessing means being hungry for His presence above all else. It means desiring more of Him, not just for what He can do for us but for who He is. When we prioritize His presence, we position ourselves to receive all the other blessings that flow from being close to Him.

In Psalm 42:1-2, the psalmist expresses this hunger: "As the deer pants for streams of water, so my soul pants for you, my God. My soul thirsts for God, for the living God. When can I go and meet with God?” This vivid imagery of a deer thirsting for water paints a picture of the kind of hunger we should have for the presence of God. Just as water is essential for life, so is the presence of God necessary for our spiritual well-being.

When we hunger for His presence, we seek Him diligently, spend time in His Word, and make room in our lives for prayer and worship. As we do, we will find that His presence brings peace, joy, wisdom, and strength. These are the true blessings that sustain us through every season of life.

How To Nurture Hunger For The Blessing

If you find that your hunger for God’s blessing has waned, it is possible to cultivate it once again. Just as the sight or smell of food can stir up physical hunger, spiritual hunger can be stirred up by spending time in God’s presence, reflecting on His promises, and hearing testimonies of His goodness.

One way to nurture hunger is to remember God's goodness in your life. Reflect on when God has blessed you, answered your prayers, or provided for your needs. This will rekindle a sense of gratitude and desire for more of His blessings. The more you focus on His goodness, the more you will want to experience it more significantly.

Another way to stir up hunger is to surround yourself with people who are passionate about God and His blessings. When you are in an environment where others seek God with intensity, it inspires you to do the same. The Bible says that iron sharpens iron (Proverbs 27:17), and being around others hungry for blessing will sharpen your desire.

You can also nurture hunger by meditating on God's promises in Scripture. As you read about the blessings God has in store for His people, your faith and expectation will grow. His Word will stir up a desire to experience His promises in your own life, and that desire will lead you to pursue the blessing with greater intensity.

Finally, hunger for blessing is a powerful force that drives us to seek God with all our hearts. It moves us from a place of complacency to a place of pursuit. Hunger is the key that unlocks the door to God's blessings in this life and the future.

You won't settle for less than God's best when hungry for a blessing. You will press through obstacles, persist in prayer, and step out in faith, knowing that God is faithful to fulfill His promises. The more you hunger for Him, the more He will fill you with His presence, favor, and abundant blessings.

Just as physical hunger causes us to seek nourishment, spiritual hunger causes us to seek God's blessings that sustain and enrich our lives. May we never lose our hunger for His presence, promises, and blessings. Let us continually pursue the fullness of what God has for us, trusting He can do far more than we could ever imagine.

Get The Blessing

Pursuing God's blessing is not just about desire; it is about taking deliberate steps to obtain it. Getting the blessing involves positioning yourself where God's favor, grace, and provision can flow into your life. It's about aligning yourself with His principles and seeking His will wholeheartedly. While hunger for the blessing is essential, hunger alone is not enough; we must actively pursue it and take hold of what God has made available to us.

In the Bible, we see countless examples of individuals who did more than desire God's blessing; they took bold steps to obtain it. These examples remind us that we must be intentional in our pursuit of the blessing and not leave it to chance. God's blessings are available, but we are responsible for pursuing them with faith, obedience, and determination.

Taking Action For The Blessing

The first key to getting the blessing is understanding that it requires action. God's blessings are not automatic; they are often the result of us stepping out in faith, obeying His instructions, and positioning ourselves to receive. Too many people miss out on the fullness of God's blessing because they are waiting passively, hoping that it will somehow fall into their laps without any effort.

In James 2:17, we are reminded that "faith by itself, if it does not have works, is dead." This means that while we must have faith in God's ability to bless us, we must also put that faith into action. If you are serious about getting the blessing, you must be willing to do whatever it takes to align yourself with God's will and purpose for your life.

Consider the story of Jacob in Genesis 32:22-30. Jacob was a man who was desperate for the blessing of God, but he didn't wait passively. He took action by wrestling with the angel of the Lord all night, refusing to let go until he received the blessing. Jacob's persistence and determination paid off, and God blessed him with a new identity and a promise of future greatness. His story teaches us that sometimes, getting the blessing requires persistence, struggle, and an unwillingness to let go until God blesses us.

Obedience And The Blessing

Another critical element in getting the blessing is obedience. God's blessings are often conditional, tied to our obedience to His Word and His will. In Deuteronomy 28:1-2, God makes this clear: "Now it shall come to pass, if you diligently obey the voice of the Lord your God, to observe all His commandments which I command you today, that the Lord your God will set you high above all nations of the earth. And all these blessings shall come upon you and overtake you because you obey the voice of the Lord your God."

Obedience opens the door to blessing. When we live in accordance with God's principles, we position ourselves to receive His favor, protection, and provision. Conversely, when we live in disobedience, we hinder the flow of God's blessings in our lives. It is not that God withholds His blessings out of punishment; rather, we remove ourselves from the path of blessing when we choose to live outside of His will.

Abraham is a perfect example of someone who received blessings through obedience. In Genesis 12, God called Abraham to leave his country, family, and father's house and go to a land He would show him. Abraham obeyed without hesitation, so God promised to make him a great nation and bless him abundantly. Abraham's obedience set him up for a lifetime of blessings, and through him, all the nations of the earth would be blessed.

Like Abraham, we must be willing to obey God's instructions, even when they seem complex or uncertain. Obedience may require sacrifice, but the following blessings are always worth it. When we choose to obey, we are choosing to trust in God's plan, and that trust opens the door to His supernatural provision.

Faith And The Blessing

Faith is another critical component in getting the blessing. Without faith, it is impossible to please God (Hebrews 11:6), and without faith, it is impossible to receive His blessings. Faith is the currency of the kingdom of God; it is how we access His promises and take hold of His blessings.

The Bible is filled with examples of people who received the blessing because of their faith. One such example is the story of the woman with the issue of blood in Mark 5:25-34. This woman had suffered for twelve long years, but her faith in Jesus' ability to heal her drove her to take action. She pressed through the crowd and touched His garment's hem, believing she would be healed. Jesus responded to her faith by telling her, "Daughter, your faith has made you well."

Faith is not just about believing in God's power to bless; it is about taking steps in line with that belief. The woman's faith led her to action, resulting in her receiving the blessing of healing. Similarly, our faith must be active to get the blessing. We must believe that God can bless us and then take steps of faith toward that blessing, even when the circumstances seem impossible.

Perseverance In The Pursuit Of The Blessing

Getting the blessing often requires perseverance. Sometimes, the blessing does not come immediately, and we must continue to press on, trusting that God is faithful to fulfill His promises. In these moments, our faith is tested, and our perseverance is refined.

The story of the persistent widow in Luke 18:1-8 is a powerful example of perseverance in the pursuit of blessing. The widow kept coming to the unjust judge, asking for justice against her adversary. Although the judge was initially unwilling, he eventually granted her request because of her persistence. Jesus used this parable to teach His disciples the importance of persevering in prayer and not giving up, even when the answer seems delayed.

Perseverance is critical to getting the blessing because it demonstrates our unwavering trust in God's timing and faithfulness. When we persist in seeking the blessing, we show God that we are serious about our desire for His favor and willing to wait on Him, no matter how long it takes.

Positioning Yourself For The Blessing

Getting the blessing also requires us to be in the correct position spiritually, emotionally, and even physically. We must be ready to receive what God has for us. This means living a life of holiness, staying connected to God through prayer and His word, and surrounding ourselves with people who encourage and uplift us in our walk with God.

In the story of Ruth, we see the importance of positioning oneself for the blessing. After the death of her husband, Ruth chose to stay with her mother-in-law, Naomi, and return to Bethlehem. Although Ruth had no guarantee of her future, she positioned herself where God could bless her. Her faithfulness and loyalty ultimately led her to Boaz, who became her redeemer and husband. Through Boaz, Ruth was blessed with a new family and future.

Ruth's story teaches us that sometimes, getting the blessing requires us to move out of our comfort zone and into unfamiliar territory. It may mean stepping out in faith and trusting God to lead us to the place where His blessing is waiting for us.

Gratitude For The Blessing

Finally, once we receive the blessing, we must respond with gratitude. Gratitude is the key to sustaining the blessing and ensuring we continue to walk in God's favor. When we are thankful for what God has done, it positions us to receive even more of His blessings in the future.

The story of the ten lepers in Luke 17:11-19 illustrates the importance of gratitude. Jesus healed all ten lepers, but only one returned to give thanks. Jesus responded by saying, "Were there not ten cleansed? But where are the nine?" The one who returned to give thanks received a more incredible blessing: He was healed, and Jesus told him, "Your faith has made you well." This suggests that his gratitude brought him to a deeper level of wholeness and blessing.

Gratitude keeps us focused on the Giver of the blessing rather than the blessing itself. It reminds us that every good and perfect gift comes from God, and it keeps our hearts in a posture of humility and dependence on Him.

Therefore, getting the blessing requires more than desire; it involves action, faith, obedience, and perseverance. God has made His blessings available to us, but we must go after them intentionally and carefully. Like Jacob, we must wrestle for the blessing, refusing to let go until God blesses us. Like Abraham, we must walk in obedience, trusting that God will fulfill His promises. And like the persistent widow, we must pray, knowing that God is faithful to answer.

As you pursue the blessing, remember that it is not just about receiving material wealth or success. The true blessing is found in a deeper relationship with God, His presence, and His favor over your life. Position yourself for the blessing, take action in faith, and trust that God will pour His blessings upon you in ways you cannot imagine.

Keep The Blessing

A blessing from God is a significant event, but it is not the journey's end. The true challenge lies in keeping the blessing. Many people receive the blessing but fail to maintain it because they do not understand the principles needed to sustain it. Just as we can lose something valuable if we do not care for it, so can the blessing slip through our hands if we do not take the necessary steps to preserve it.

In life, the enemy seeks to steal, kill, and destroy (John 10:10). Once you receive a blessing, the enemy often intensifies his efforts to disrupt your life, pull you away from the source of the blessing, and rob you of what God has given. Therefore, keeping the blessing requires spiritual diligence, careful stewardship, and a commitment to the principles that led to it in the first place.

Guard The Blessing Through Obedience

The first and most important way to keep the blessing is through continued obedience to God's word. Obedience is not just the key to receiving the blessing but also the key to maintaining it. Once we begin to walk in the blessing, we must be careful not to become complacent or take it for granted. God's commands are not meant to be followed only when we are seeking His favor; they must be obeyed consistently.

In Deuteronomy 28, God promised the Israelites that if they obeyed His commands, blessings would come upon them and overtake them. However, in the same chapter, He warned that disobedience would lead to curses, and the blessings they enjoyed would be removed. This shows us that obedience is not a one-time event but a lifelong commitment. Keeping the blessing requires us to remain faithful to God, even after the blessing has been received.

King Saul in the Bible is an example of someone who received the blessing of kingship but failed to keep it because of disobedience. God chose Saul to be the first king of Israel and blessed him with authority, success, and favor. However, Saul disobeyed God's instructions, so the blessing of kingship was removed from him and given to David (1 Samuel 15). Saul's story teaches us that we must be careful to maintain the attitude of obedience that initially brought the blessing into our lives.

Stay Humble Amid The Blessing

Another important principle for keeping the blessing is humility. When God blesses us, it can be tempting to become proud or self-reliant. We might start to believe that the blessing results from our efforts rather than God's grace. Pride is dangerous because it separates us from God; without God, we cannot sustain the blessing.

In Proverbs 16:18, we are warned that "pride goes before destruction and a haughty spirit before a fall." Pride not only leads to the loss of the blessing but also sets us up for failure in other areas of our lives. To keep the blessing, we must stay humble and recognize that every good thing in our lives comes from God (James 1:17). We must remain in a posture of gratitude and dependence on Him, acknowledging that we need His guidance and strength to maintain what He has given us.

King Nebuchadnezzar is a powerful example of how pride can lead to the loss of the blessing. In Daniel 4, Nebuchadnezzar was a powerful king with wealth, authority, and success. However, he became proud and attributed his success to his abilities. As a result, God humbled him by removing the blessing of his kingship for some time. Nebuchadnezzar lost everything until he acknowledged that God gave him the blessing. Only then was his kingship restored.

Humility keeps us grounded and connected to the source of blessing. It reminds us that we can do nothing without God and positions us to continue walking in His favor.

Steward The Blessing Wisely

Keeping the blessing also requires wise stewardship. When God blesses us with resources, opportunities, or influence, He expects us to manage them well. Stewardship means taking responsibility for the blessing and using it to honor God and align with His purposes. It is not enough to receive the blessing; we must be faithful in handling it.

In Matthew 25:14-30, Jesus told the parable of the talents, where a master entrusted his servants with different amounts of money to manage while he was away. The servants who wisely invested and multiplied their talents were rewarded, while those who hid their talent and failed to use it lost everything. This parable teaches us that God expects us to be good stewards of what He gives us. If we squander the blessing or fail to use it for His glory, we risk losing it.

Wise stewardship involves managing the spiritual and material blessings God has given us. It means using our time, talents, and resources to advance God's kingdom and help others. When we steward the blessing well, we demonstrate to God that we are trustworthy, and He often entrusts us with even more.

Protect The Blessing Through Prayer

Prayer is another essential element in keeping the blessing. Once we receive the blessing, we must cover it in prayer and ask God for His continued protection and guidance. The enemy is always looking for ways to disrupt our lives and steal what God has given us, but through prayer, we can guard against his attacks.

In Ephesians 6:18, we are encouraged to "pray in the Spirit on all occasions with all kinds of prayers and requests." This includes praying for the strength to maintain the blessing and for wisdom in stewarding it. Prayer keeps us connected to God and our hearts aligned with His will. Through prayer, we receive the guidance, strength, and protection we need to keep walking in the blessing.

King David is an excellent example of someone who consistently prayed to protect and maintain the blessings in his life. David faced many challenges before and after becoming king but constantly prayed to God. Whether seeking guidance, protection, or strength, David understood that prayer was vital to staying in God's favor and maintaining the blessings he had received.

Stay Connected To The Source Of The Blessing

To keep the blessing, we must stay connected to its source, God Himself. When we disconnect from God, we disconnect from His blessings flow. This is why it is so essential to maintain a close, intimate relationship with Him through prayer, worship, and the study of His Word.

Jesus teaches us in John 15:5 that "I am the vine, you are the branches. He who abides in Me, and I in him, bears much fruit; for without Me you can do nothing." This scripture reminds us that our ability to keep the blessing is directly tied to our connection with Jesus. If we remain in Him, we will continue to bear fruit and walk in His blessings. However, if we drift away from Him, we cut ourselves from the very source of life and blessing.

Staying connected to God means prioritizing your relationship with Him above everything else. It means making time for prayer, worship, and studying His Word, even amid busy seasons. It means staying sensitive to the Holy Spirit's leading and being quick to repent if you fall into sin. When we stay close to God, His blessings will continue to flow in our lives.

Be Grateful For The Blessing

Gratitude is a powerful key to keeping the blessing. When we express gratitude for what God has done, we acknowledge His goodness and faithfulness. Gratitude keeps our hearts in the correct posture and reminds us that the blessing is a gift from God, not something we earn on our own.

In 1 Thessalonians 5:18, we are instructed to "give thanks in all circumstances; for this is God's will for you in Christ Jesus." A grateful heart recognizes the source of the blessing and continues to rely on God's grace to sustain it. When we thank God for what He has done, it allows even more blessings to flow into our lives.

Consider the Israelites' example in the wilderness. After God delivered them from Egypt and miraculously provided for them, many of them quickly forgot His blessings and began to grumble and complain. Their lack of gratitude led to their downfall, and many never entered the Promised Land. In contrast, those who remained grateful and trusted in God could receive and keep His promised blessings.

Keeping the blessing is not passive; it requires intentionality, faithfulness, and a heart that remains aligned with God's will. Through continued obedience, humility, wise stewardship, and prayer, we can protect and maintain God's blessings in our lives.

Remember that the blessing is not just for you; it is meant to overflow into the lives of others and bring glory to God. As you keep the blessing, continue to seek ways to use it to bless those around you, and trust that God will multiply it in ways beyond your imagination.

Distribute The Blessing

Receiving a blessing from God is a great experience, but the true essence of the blessing is not just accepting it but sharing it with others. God's blessings are not meant to be hoarded or kept to ourselves; they are designed to flow through us and impact the lives of those around us. When distributing the blessing, we act as channels of God's grace, extending His favor and goodness to those in need.

The principle of distributing blessings is rooted in God's very nature, who gives generously and freely to all. James 1:17 says, "Every good gift and every perfect gift is from above, and comes down from the Father of lights." God's gifts are meant to be shared, and when we distribute His blessings, we align ourselves with His heart and His purpose for the world.

Blessing Others Is An Act Of Obedience

One of the primary reasons we should distribute the blessing is because it is an act of obedience to God. Throughout Scripture, we see that God commands us to be generous and to care for those in need. In Luke 6:38, Jesus tells us, "Give, and it will be given to you: good measure, pressed down, shaken together, and running over will be put into your bosom." This verse highlights the importance of giving, not just for the sake of receiving more, but because it reflects the heart of God.

When we distribute the blessing, we obey God's command to love our neighbors as ourselves (Mark 12:31). The blessings we receive are not meant to create a sense of superiority or self-sufficiency but to enable us to help others. Obedience in distributing the blessing keeps us humble, reminding us that everything we have comes from God and that we are stewards of His grace.

Consider the example of the early church in Acts 2:44-45, where believers sold their possessions and goods to give to anyone in need. This community understood that their blessings were not just for their benefit but should be shared with others. Their obedience to God's call to be generous resulted in a powerful display of unity, love, and God's provision for everyone.

Blessing Others Reflects God's Love

When distributing the blessing, we reflect God's love to the world. God's love is selfless, giving, and overflowing, and as His children, we are called to demonstrate that same love to others. Distributing the blessing allows us to be a tangible expression of God's love, showing people that He cares for their needs and desires to bless them through us.

In Matthew 5:16, Jesus encourages us to "let your light so shine before men, that they may see your good works and glorify your Father in heaven." When we bless others, we are not seeking personal recognition or accolades; instead, we point them to the ultimate source of all blessings, God Himself. Our acts of kindness and generosity become a testimony to God's love and goodness, drawing people closer to Him.

One of the best ways to reflect God's love is by meeting the practical needs of those around us. Whether providing financial assistance, encouragement, or our time and resources, distributing the blessing allows us to make a meaningful impact on others. When we respond to the needs of others with compassion and generosity, we demonstrate the heart of Christ, who came not to be served but to serve (Mark 10:45).

Distributing The Blessing Multiplies It

Another important aspect of distributing blessings is that they multiply. The more we give, the more we open ourselves up to receiving even greater blessings from God. This principle is not about selfish gain but about understanding that God blesses us so that we can continue to bless others. The cycle of blessing and giving creates a flow of abundance that impacts not only our lives but also the lives of those around us.

In 2 Corinthians 9:6-8, Apostle Paul teaches, "He who sows sparingly will also reap sparingly, and he who sows bountifully will also reap bountifully. So let each one give as he purposes in his heart, not grudgingly or of necessity; for God loves a cheerful giver." This passage reveals that when we give generously, God responds by providing for us abundantly so that we can continue to do good works.

Distributing the blessing is like planting seeds. When we sow seeds of generosity, kindness, and compassion, we reap a harvest of blessings in return. These blessings may not always come in material wealth, but they could manifest as peace, joy, favor, or opportunities to impact others further. The more we give, the more we align ourselves with God's economy of abundance, where there is always enough to meet every need.

Distribute The Blessing With A Pure Heart

While distributing the blessing is necessary, the attitude with which we do it is equally important. God is concerned not just with our actions but with the condition of our hearts. We should distribute the blessing with a pure heart, not out of obligation or to gain recognition, but out of love for God and a desire to serve others.

In 2 Corinthians 9:7, we are reminded that "God loves a cheerful giver." Our giving should be joyful and willing, not grudgingly or under compulsion. When we give with a pure heart, we honor God and reflect His character. A pure heart also means giving without expecting anything in return. Our motivation should be to glorify God and bless others, trusting that God will care for our needs.

Jesus is the ultimate example of selfless giving. He gave His life for us not because He had to but because He wanted to. His love for humanity was so great that He willingly laid down His life so we could experience eternal life's blessing. As we distribute the blessing to others, we should do so with the same selfless love and humility that Jesus demonstrated.

Distribute The Blessing To Those In Need

One of the primary ways we can distribute the blessing is by helping those in need. Throughout the Bible, we see God's heart for the poor, the widows, the orphans, and the marginalized. In James 1:27, we are told that "pure and undefiled religion before God and the Father is this: to visit orphans and widows in their trouble, and to keep oneself unspotted from the world." This verse signifies the importance of caring for those who are vulnerable and in need.

When we distribute the blessing to those in need, we become Jesus' hands and feet, ministering to their physical and spiritual needs. Jesus Himself said, "Whatever you did for one of the least of these brothers and sisters of mine, you did for me" (Matthew 25:40). Our acts of generosity toward those in need reflect our love for Christ and our desire to honor Him.

It's essential to recognize that distributing the blessing to those in need is not limited to material resources. While financial assistance is necessary, we can bless others in many ways. We can offer our time, our skills, and our prayers. Sometimes, a listening ear or a word of encouragement can be just as valuable as financial support. The key is to be attentive to the needs around us and to respond with a heart of compassion.

Distribute The Blessing In The Marketplace

Another way to distribute the blessing is by using the influence and resources God has given us in the marketplace. Whether we are business owners, employees, or leaders in our communities, we can impact others through our work. God can use our businesses, careers, and leadership positions as platforms to distribute His blessings.

We can distribute the blessing in the marketplace by treating others with kindness, fairness, and integrity. We can create opportunities for others to thrive through employment, mentorship, or partnerships. By operating with godly principles and a heart of generosity, we can be a light in the marketplace and extend God's blessings to those we interact with.

In the Old Testament, Joseph is an excellent example of someone who distributed the blessing in the marketplace. Even though he faced many challenges, Joseph remained faithful to God. As a result, he could distribute the blessings of wisdom, leadership, and provision to the people of Egypt and beyond. His influence extended far beyond his personal life, impacting an entire nation and preserving the lives of many during a time of famine (Genesis 41:56-57).

Distributing the blessing is not just a responsibility; it is a privilege. When we allow God's blessings to flow through us, we become conduits of His love, grace, and provision to a needy world. As we distribute the blessing, we fulfill God's purpose for our lives, bringing glory to His name and impacting the lives of others in profound ways.

Remember that the blessings we receive are not meant to be kept to ourselves. God has blessed us so that we can be a blessing to others. As we distribute the blessing with a pure heart, in obedience to God's Word, and with a desire to reflect His love, we will experience the joy of being part of His redemptive work in the world.

CHAPTER FIVE

EVERYDAY BLESSINGS TO BE THANKFUL FOR

As we journey through life, it's easy to become focused on the challenges we face and the things we lack. However, the Bible calls us to cultivate a heart of gratitude, recognizing and giving thanks for God's blessings. Often, the blessings we take for granted are the ones that sustain us the most. This chapter will reflect on eight everyday blessings that are often overlooked but vital to our well-being, growth, and fulfillment.

The Blessing Of Health

One of the most undervalued blessings is health. Many people only realize how valuable health is when they lose it. Good health is a gift from God, allowing us to live our lives to the fullest, pursue our dreams, and fulfill our purpose. Without health, even the simplest tasks become difficult, and our capacity to serve God and others is diminished.

Psalm 103:2-3 says, "Bless the Lord, O my soul, and forget not all His benefits: who forgives all your iniquities, who heals all your diseases." This passage reminds us that God's blessings include spiritual benefits, physical health, and healing. It's important to thank God for the gift of health every day, whether in perfect health or experiencing illness. Each day, we wake up and can move, breathe, and function, a blessing.

Being thankful for health also encourages us to be good stewards of our bodies. As 1 Corinthians 6:19-20 teaches, our bodies are temples of the Holy Spirit, and we should honor God with how we care for them. When we recognize health as a blessing, we are more likely to take care of ourselves, make wise decisions, and avoid habits that could harm our bodies.

The Gift Of Relationships

Another common blessing often taken for granted is the gift of relationships. God has designed us to live in community, and our relationships with family, friends, and others are essential to our lives. These relationships provide us with support, encouragement, love, and companionship.

When did you last thank God for the relationships He has given you? Whether it's a spouse, a friend, a parent, or a mentor, the people in our lives are gifts from God. Ecclesiastes 4:9-10 reminds us, "Two are better than one because they have a good reward for their labor. For if they fall, one will lift his companion." Relationships strengthen and help us grow in our faith and character.

Healthy relationships reflect God's love for us. In John 15:12, Jesus commands us to "love one another as I have loved you." Through our relationships, we can experience and share God's love. Therefore, it is essential to be thankful for the people God has placed in our lives and to invest time and effort into nurturing those relationships.

The Blessing Of Salvation

Salvation is perhaps the most profound and life-changing blessing we can receive. We are reconciled to God through salvation, the forgiveness of our sins, and the promise of eternal life. Romans 8:15 (AMP) tells us, "For you have not received a spirit of slavery leading again to fear, but you have received the Spirit of adoption as sons, by which we cry out, 'Abba! Father!'" This scripture reveals the depth of the relationship we gain through salvation, a personal, intimate connection with God as our Father.

The gift of salvation is not something we can earn; God gives it freely through His grace. Ephesians 2:8-9 reminds us, "For by grace you have been saved through faith, and that not of yourselves; it is the gift of God, not of works, lest anyone should boast." Our salvation is a blessing we must never take for granted. It is the foundation of our relationship with God and the key to living a life of purpose and fulfillment.

Thankfulness for salvation should be at the core of our daily lives. Every day, we should thank God for the sacrifice of Jesus Christ, which made our salvation possible. Additionally, gratitude for our salvation should motivate us to share the good news with others so that they, too, can experience the blessing of eternal life.

The Gift Of Companionship

Companionship is another vital blessing that brings comfort, joy, and strength to our lives. God, in His love, has not left us alone in this world; He has given us the Holy Spirit as our constant companion. John 14:26 (AMP) says, "But the Helper (Comforter, Advocate, Intercessor – Counselor, Strengthener, Standby), the Holy Spirit, whom the Father will send in My name, He will teach you all things, and He will help you remember everything that I have told you."

The Holy Spirit is a faithful companion who guides, teaches, and empowers us to live according to God's will. This gift of companionship is not limited to human relationships but extends to a divine partnership with God Himself. Knowing we are never alone is a blessing, even in the most challenging times.

In addition to the Holy Spirit, God also blesses us with human companions. Whether it's a spouse, close friends, or fellow believers, companionship enriches our lives and provides us with the emotional and spiritual support we need. We must be intentional about expressing gratitude for the companionship God has provided, both through His Spirit and through the people He has placed in our lives.

The Blessing Of Stable Finances

Financial stability is a blessing many overlook, especially in a world where materialism and pursuing wealth often overshadow contentment and gratitude. However, having enough to meet our needs, provide for our families, and contribute to God's kingdom is a significant blessing. Philippians 4:19 assures us, "And my God shall supply all your need according to His riches in glory by Christ Jesus."

While financial blessings may vary from person to person, it's important to remember that God is our ultimate provider. The ability to work, earn an income, and manage our finances wisely are gifts from God. Gratitude for financial stability should lead us to be good stewards of our resources, using them to bless others and advance the work of God's kingdom.

In addition, financial stability allows us to live without the constant worry of lack. In Matthew 6:31-33, Jesus reminds us not to worry about what we eat, drink, or wear because our Heavenly Father knows our needs and will provide for us. When we trust God as our provider and are thankful for our financial blessings, we can experience peace and contentment.

The Spirit Of Creativity

Creativity is a unique blessing that allows us to reflect the image of God, the ultimate Creator. Whether through art, music, writing, problem-solving, or innovation, the ability to create is a gift that brings joy and fulfillment to our lives. Genesis 1:27 tells us that we are made in God's image, and part of that image includes the ability to create and bring new things into existence.

Thankfulness for the spirit of creativity should inspire us to use our gifts to glorify God and bless others. Whether it's through creating something beautiful or finding creative solutions to challenges, our creativity can positively impact the world around us. Colossians 3:23 encourages us, "And whatever you do, do it heartily, as to the Lord and not to men." When we use our creativity with gratitude, we honor God and contribute to His work.

The Gift Of Provision

God is a faithful provider who meets our needs according to His perfect will. The gift of provision is one of the most common blessings we experience daily, whether it's food, shelter, clothing, or other necessities. In Matthew 6:11, Jesus teaches us to pray, "Give us this day our daily bread." This simple prayer reminds us that everything comes from God, and we should be thankful for His provision daily.

The gift of provision is about having enough to survive and recognizing that God cares for every detail of our lives. He knows our needs before we ask and delights in providing for His children. Gratitude for God's provision should lead us to trust Him more fully, knowing He will always care for us.

The Ability To Love And Be Loved

Finally, one of our most precious blessings is the ability to love and be loved. Love is the essence of who God is, and as His children, we are called to reflect that love in our relationships with others. 1 John 4:19 says, "We love Him because He first loved us." Our ability to love comes from God; through His love, we can form deep, meaningful connections with others.

Giving and receiving love is a blessing that enriches our lives in countless ways. Love brings joy, comfort, and fulfillment, whether it's the love of family, friends, or a spouse. As we express gratitude for the ability to love and be loved, we also acknowledge God's greatest act of love, God's love for us through Jesus Christ.

In conclusion, these eight everyday blessings are gifts from God for which we should be thankful every day. When we develop a heart of gratitude, we shift our focus from what we lack to the abundance of blessings we already have. Gratitude opens our eyes to God's goodness and helps us live with joy and contentment, trusting that He will continue to bless and provide for us every season.

CONCLUSION

As I conclude this book on The Commanded Blessing, we must reflect on the truths we have uncovered in the book. The commanded blessing is not merely an abstract concept; it is a tangible reality that can transform our lives when we align ourselves with God's purpose and actively pursue the blessings He has promised us.

From understanding the various types of blessings, whether from our biological parents, spiritual fathers, families, or the Lord Himself, we have seen how each blessing serves a unique purpose. Each blessing can propel us forward, sustain us through life's challenges, and ultimately lead us to a place of abundance and fulfillment.

We have explored our responsibilities in receiving and maintaining these blessings, emphasizing the importance of diligently seeking them, nurturing a hunger for God's blessings, and being good stewards of what we receive. Our journey has highlighted the necessity of gratitude, as acknowledging our blessings enables us to experience joy and contentment, even amid trials.

Similarly, we have been reminded of the blessings that we often take for granted: the gift of health, relationships, salvation, companionship, financial stability, creativity, provision, and the ability to love. These blessings enrich our lives and reflect God's goodness and faithfulness. As we develop a heart of gratitude, we recognize that every good thing in our lives comes from Him, urging us to share our blessings with others and to create a ripple effect of love and generosity in our communities.

The commanded blessing is a divine enablement, a supernatural empowerment that accompanies those who obey God's word. It transcends circumstances, challenges, and obstacles. When we embrace the commanded blessing, we invite God's favor and presence into our lives, equipping us to fulfill our God-given purpose and impacting the world around us.

As we conclude this book, I encourage you to reflect on the blessings in your life and commit to embracing them wholeheartedly. Seek the Lord in prayer, asking Him to reveal areas where you can deepen your understanding of His blessings and your responsibility to maintain and distribute them. Let gratitude fill your heart and inspire your actions as you engage with those around you, sharing the blessings you have received.

Remember, the commanded blessing is not just for you; it is meant to flow through you to bless others. May you live in a manner that glorifies God, honors the blessings He has given you, and impacts the lives of those you encounter. As we walk in the light of His blessing, we become vessels of His grace and love, demonstrating the power of a life aligned with God's will.

In the days ahead, may you continue to experience the fullness of God's commanded blessing in every aspect of your life, knowing that His desire is for you to thrive, succeed, and fulfill the purpose He has ordained for you. Embrace the commanded blessing, for it is the key to proliferation and sustenance, allowing you to flourish every season. Let us go forth, empowered by the commanded blessing, to bring hope, healing, and transformation to our world.

A SPECIAL CALL TO SALVATION & NEW BEGINNINGS FROM APOSTLE DR. DAVID PHILEMON

Dear Beloved,

God loves you deeply and has brought you to this moment for a reason. No matter your past, His love and forgiveness are available to you.

The Bible says in John 3:16, "For God so loved the world that He gave His one and only Son, that whoever believes in Him shall not perish but have eternal life." Jesus Christ came to save you, offering you a new life of purpose and peace.

If you're ready to accept Jesus as your Lord and Savior, pray this simple prayer:

The Salvation Prayer

"Heavenly Father, I come to You in the Name of Jesus. I acknowledge that I am a sinner in need of a Savior. I believe that Jesus Christ is Your Son, that He died for my sins, and that You raised Him from the dead. I repent of my sins and turn to You with

my
Whole heart. Jesus, I ask You to come into my life. Be my Lord and my Savior. I surrender my life to You. Fill me with Your Holy Spirit, guide me on the path of righteousness, and help me to follow Your script for my life. Thank you, Father, for saving me. In the name of Jesus. Amen."

Welcome to the Family of God!

If you have just prayed this prayer, Congratulations! You are now a child of God, and heaven is rejoicing. Your journey has begun, and we're here to support you as you grow in faith and discover God's unique plans for you.

Next Steps:

• Connect with a Bible-believing church.
• Read the Bible Daily: God's Word is your guide.
• Pray Regularly: Prayer is your lifeline to God.
• Share Your Faith: Don't keep the good news to yourself.

www.ingramcontent.com/pod-product-compliance
Lightning Source LLC
Chambersburg PA
CBHW071903020426
42331CB00010B/2643
9781966141204